Two Young Dancers
Their World of Ballet

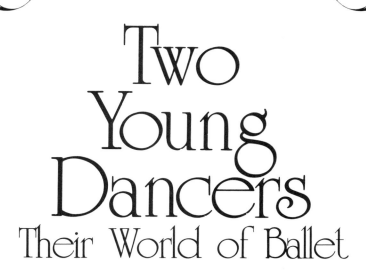

Two Young Dancers
Their World of Ballet

Alexandra Collard

Photographs by Frank Dunand, Doug Magee,
and Tom Hohing

Julian Messner  New York

In memory of my mother,
Nan Carpenter,
with love.

Copyright © 1984 by Alexandra Collard

Published by Julian Messner,
A Division of Simon & Schuster, Inc.
Simon & Schuster Building,
1230 Avenue of the Americas,
New York, New York 10020.
JULIAN MESSNER and colophon are trademarks of
Simon & Schuster, Inc.

10 9 8 7 6 5 4 3 2 1

Manufactured in the United States of America

Design by Beverly Haw Leung, A Good Thing, Inc.

Library of Congress Cataloging in Publication Data.

Collard, Alexandra.
    2 young dancers.

    Includes index.
    Summary: Two fifteen-year-old American ballet students,
a boy and a girl, discuss their training, their lives
and experiences as performers, and their hopes for
ballet stardom.
    1. Gregory, Shane—Juvenile literature. 2. Colgate,
Melissa—Juvenile literature. 3. Ballet dancers—United
States—Biography—Juvenile literature. [1. Gregory,
Shane. 2. Colgate, Melissa. 3. Dancers. 4. Ballet
dancing. 5. Ballet] I. Dunand, Frank, ill. II. Title.
III. Title: Two young dancers.
GV1785.A1C6   1984   792.8'2'0922 [B] [920]   83-26435
ISBN 0-671-47074-4

CONTENTS

INTRODUCTION

Shane Gregory and Melissa Colgate are approaching the most critical time in their young lives. Both of them have recently had their fifteenth birthdays, and they know that at the most two years remain before they will either be welcomed or rejected by a major ballet company.

Only a handful of major ballet companies exist in the United States. Each company has about sixty dancers who are chosen from thousands who audition every year. To train for years with the slim hope of getting into one of these companies is a huge undertaking, but Shane and Melissa are determined and willing to try.

These two teenagers never met until last year. Now they attend the same academic school and share a group of friends in the arts.

Shane is from California. His parents were divorced when he was younger, and he and his sister, Stephanie, were raised by their mother. She was a costumer and stage manager, among other things. Shane loved all the lights and excitement of the theater. By the age of eleven, he was a working performer himself.

Melissa grew up in the East. Her family spent a short time in California and then returned to New Jersey so Melissa could become a dancer. The most exciting moment in her life was when, at the age of thirteen, she was talked into going to an audition for

the American Ballet Theatre first company. She was kept until the end of the class and was chosen by Mikhail Baryshnikov to be one of his twelve scholarship students.

Shane's and Melissa's lives have been filled with stars and glamour, but there have been times of frustration and anxiety also. Shane and Melissa are not child wonders, or the children of celebrities. They did not realize the extent of their careers until two years ago, when they arrived in New York City to face what might be the greatest challenge they will ever face.

This is not just the story of Shane and Melissa. It is the story of thousands of other young people with the same dream. This is not a "Cinderella" book, and it has an uncertain ending. But Shane and Melissa are fighters, and whatever becomes of them, they will be stronger for having tried.

SHANE

The Early Years

I was born in West Germany in a place called the Mosel River Valley. Someday I would like to go back there and see it because it's supposed to be beautiful, with huge castles on the cliff tops.

Since I was born there, my citizenship is half German, but both my parents are American. I would probably have no trouble getting into a German ballet company, but I could also be drafted into the West German army.

My father was a fighter pilot, and my mother was what you would call a theater person. She was a costumer and stage manager when she wasn't onstage dancing, singing, or acting.

I never got to know Germany. When I was a year and a half old, Dad left the military. We moved to Southern California and Mom left Dad. I was too young to understand about divorce then, but I do remember I was very sad for a while.

Luckily, I didn't have much time to think about that. My younger sister, Stephanie, and I traveled all over the world with Mom visiting exciting places like England, Australia, New Zealand, the Greek islands, and France. While in London, I went to nursery school. Before long I was talking like a little English kid, calling my mother "Mum" and singing songs about a fisherman who caught a "jolly big fish." The thing I loved the most about London was riding around in the double-decker buses.

All through our travels, my sister and I were part of a strange adult world. We used to spend hours backstage in different theaters, surrounded by scenery, theater cases, and stage props while Mom worked. Whenever we were left on our own, we were always given strict instructions not to cause any trouble and to be absolutely quiet. During performances we stayed in the dressing room with hundreds of costumes hanging over our heads. The only thing we had was a coloring book. I never colored so much in my life. Stephanie still draws and paints. She says she wants to be a veterinarian or an artist. I want to be a ballet dancer in a major company.

There was more theater in our lives than dance during our world travels. Like most kids I only remember the really crazy parts of our trips, such as the time I fell down a sheep slide in Australia and landed face to face with a sheared lamb. I don't know which one of us was more scared. All I know is that I started screaming, and the sheep rancher had to pull me out.

In Greece, Stephanie and I got chased by a farmer with a pitchfork because we were playing in his hay pile. I also remember riding on the neighbor's donkey through the olive groves. Once the saddle came off, and my sister and I fell under the donkey's stomach.

I don't remember too much about the theaters except that they all looked alike. I didn't really get interested in ballet until we settled in California. I was about seven years old. Stephanie had begun ballet lessons, and I was a forward on the school soccer team. Unfortunately, we never won a game, but I had fun.

It was strange that my sister was the one who began dance classes, because I was the one most anxious to be onstage. One reason I got into soccer was that the boys in our neighborhood were into sports. So I went along with the crowd.

My real desire to start taking dance lessons came when we took Stephanie to an audition for the *Nutcracker*. She was trying out for a part as one of the

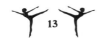

gingerbread children. She was also competing with two hundred other little girls just as good as she was. Only three boys were there. One of them could hardly do anything, but he got a part. I realized that there were not many boys in ballet, and those that were could get into anything they wanted.

But Mom knew it was not that easy. When I asked her if I could study ballet, she said no. I kept at her for almost a year, asking if I could just take one lesson. Stephanie hated dance and wanted to be an ice skater or a gymnast. But I was really interested in ballet and was determined to get in somehow.

I guess Mom finally decided I was serious, since she bought me a pair of tights and ballet shoes and drove me to an evaluation class with her own dance instructor, a nice English lady named Lynn Hodgkinson. Miss Hodgkinson was trained at the Royal Ballet School in London and would not allow any fooling around in class. She rarely praised anyone for anything unless the person was sensational. Her highest form of a compliment was usually "That's better."

I took the children's primary class, which was already completing its first year of training in the Royal Academy Syllabus. This is a set of rules and steps for beginning training—sort of like a first-grade textbook for dance. For some reason, I had very little trouble keeping up. But I did feel kind of stupid. Here I was with all these little girls in white leotards and pink headbands. They were all staring at me and giggling. I was forced to learn the steps just to keep from looking like an idiot; when I did learn them, the girls seemed to respect me. Some of them even tried to make friends. One of the girls from the academy is still a friend of mine.

After the trial class, Miss Hodgkinson went out and told Mom that I had real potential and she was eager to work with me. Since Mom knew this was not just flattery, she agreed to let me continue my dance studies.

Everyone told me I took on ballet like it was the most serious thing in my life. It *was*—at that time and now. Miss Hodgkinson used to comment to my mom on how I analyzed the steps she gave us. I would stand there pointing and flexing my foot to feel the different muscles and try to understand what was happening inside my arch. Sometimes this action would put me several beats behind the music, and I would get in the way of the girls on either side of me.

Each of us was given a dictionary of ballet terms. We were told to study them and learn several each week. Miss Hodgkinson was always quizzing us because the following spring we had to take the Queen's Exams for the Royal Academy of Dance. This is a graded series of tests where you show how much you know by demonstrating different steps and performing a three-minute dance. The girls were allowed to perform in pairs, but because I had to do a special boy's dance, I was going to dance alone. Miss Hodgkinson did not think I wanted to be a shepherdess or a wood fairy, so she choreographed a dance about a boy splashing around in puddles after a rainstorm. It gave me the oppportunity to show off how well I could jump. Jumping was always one of my stronger points.

The examiner was flown over from England. We were expected to wear a particular uniform. My biggest problem was trying to figure out what to wear under my black tights. I had been wearing white jockey shorts and they looked terrible. What I really wanted was a dance belt. This is like an athletic supporter, but they don't make them for eight-year-old boys. After searching every shopping mall in the city, I found a pair of navy-blue jockey shorts, which looked all right.

The other problem was my hair. It was too long and shaggy, but I didn't want to get it cut short. I was already having enough problems with my classmates in academic school who thought I was crazy to be studying ballet. They would spin around in stupid little circles, waving their arms, and tell me how dumb ballet was and how easy to do. They didn't know anything, and the way they pretended to dance really made me angry. We solved the hair problem with a headband, the kind tennis players wear. In this way I was able to look all right for the examiner and still look like a California beach boy.

Something I have always noticed about California and the people who live there is how important looks are. People think that Californians are blond and look very athletic. Most Californians really do try to look that way, and they get teased a lot by their friends if they don't. This is especially true in the beach towns like the one where I lived. But I guess Californians aren't the only ones who act that way.

When I took the exams, the examiner sat at a table in the studio. She smiled and seemed nice, but I started perspiring even before I danced a step. Having to dance alone didn't help either. All of a sudden, the studio seemed enormous. I had worked there by myself with Miss Hodgkinson, but being in there with an examiner was a whole different thing. What worried me the most was that I'd forget everything. I could just see the examiner asking me to show the positions of the feet, and I would not remember what they were. But somehow I got through everything, even the dance, which was just as much mime as ballet. I had to wait six weeks for the results.

On the day of the awards we had a special class. Mom had to work, so my dad came to watch. He didn't know anything about ballet but he always supported me. I guess I was lucky that way because lots of other boys who dance have a lot of trouble convincing their dads that it is not just a dumb hobby and that it is a very athletic thing to do. Some adults actually think boys wear toe shoes and tutus!

The awards given out ranged from pass to commended to highly commended to honors. No one had failed. I didn't know what to expect. I had two reasons for feeling anxious. I wanted Dad to be proud of what I was doing. And I felt this was the first measure of my future in dance. If I did badly, Mom would have been right to keep me out of dance. But if I did well, then I would feel like I should continue, and that ballet was a good choice. Being the only boy, I was always favored in places like San Diego, but the examiner had seen lots of boys. I was just another one to her. So I waited there and, as they say, I had my stomach in my mouth. Then my name was called. "Shane Gregory, honors." I got honors!

The moment I received the award I knew I had to be a dancer, a great classical ballet dancer. I looked across the studio at a poster on the wall. It was a picture of Nureyev, my idol at the time. I wanted to be like him, the best in the world. When future theater-goers would talk about ballet, they would also talk about Shane Gregory. I was going to dance all over the world.

I was eight years old then and had a lot to learn about getting there.

That same spring, the American Ballet Theatre company was in Los Angeles doing their seasonal engagement at the Dorothy Chandler Pavilion. Of all the major companies, they are the most lyrical, which means they dance more of the well-known ballets like *Swan Lake* and the *Nutcracker*. Mom got tickets for *Swan Lake*. She couldn't believe that I could sit through three hours of dance with a pair of binoculars and not be bored or restless. I was fascinated. All the things I was trying to learn came to life onstage. It was an exciting ballet with von Rothbart in his hawk costume and smoke and the Black Swan trying to trick the prince into thinking she was the White Swan and the most beautiful music I ever heard in my life. I was so fascinated by the ballet that Mom bought tickets to another ballet called *La Sylphide*.

I loved that ballet too, even though some of it was a little silly, like when the sylphs (which are fairy-like creatures) were out in the forest running around the man. Ivan Nagy danced the lead role of James. He is a dancer from Hungary who does the most perfect grand jeté (split in the air) I have ever seen. The ballerina was Natalia Makarova, who was originally from Russia. She was so light on her toes that I almost believed she had real wings.

We also saw *Billy the Kid*, which has always been one of my favorites. I still dream of dancing the role of Billy someday. To me, the role of Billy is like the role of the Swan Queen to some girls. After the performance we went backstage and I met John Prinz. He was a principal dancer for American Ballet Theatre. He was also one of Makarova's first partners after she left

Russia. He told me he had attended the School of American Ballet in New York City. He said that if I was really serious about becoming a dancer, I would eventually have to win a scholarship and go there. But he also said boys have a lot of competition in New York. I listened to what he told me and decided that someday I was going to New York. Someday soon.

By the end of that summer of 1975, casting began again for the *Nutcracker*. Only a few boys auditioned. I discovered later that even then the New York City Ballet, which is one of the largest companies in the United States, used girls in boys' roles. But at that time the New York City Ballet was a long way off for me.

I made the mistake of auditioning for a small local company and was cast as Fritz, the little brother who breaks the nutcracker doll. But after I auditioned, I realized I wanted to dance with another company that was larger and was going to perform in the Civic Theatre, a beautiful place like the Dorothy Chandler in Los Angeles. The large company also used a full orchestra instead of taped music. Mom checked the performance schedules and discovered that they did not clash at any time, so I auditioned for the larger company too.

The audition itself was ridiculous. They just lined up all the boys and taught us a simple dance that we performed with the girls who had already been selected. Television cameras were there, along with about two hundred ballet mothers who kept straightening their daughters' hair ribbons and baggy leotards. My mom was there, but she was auditioning too, so she did little more than watch me from a corner where she was warming up. We were both cast

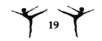

19

I got the role of Fritz, the little brother, in my first *Nutcracker*.

in the two productions. This was convenient because Mom had to drive me to rehearsals anyway. What we didn't count on was an overlap in rehearsal schedules of the two companies. As we got closer to Christmas, Mom and I were literally running in full stage make-up from the performance of one company to the rehearsal of the other.

I'll never forget the first dress rehearsal with the orchestra onstage at the Civic Theatre. I looked out at the empty seats. They seemed to go on for miles. I kept thinking, there are going to be people in all those seats, all staring at us. This was different from the performances in high school auditoriums and gymnasiums with audiences of fifteen, half of them people's parents.

Even with that large scary theater, I don't remember having stage fright once I began to perform. A lot of people have told me I look very much at home onstage, and I think the main reason is that I am not afraid. Once I'm in front of the lights, I try to get into whatever role I am doing and I'm only aware of the audience when I hear laughter or applause. Of course, most of my roles have been more mime than dance. I guess if I had to go out and do a difficult solo dance, I would probably be terrified.

In 1976, Miss Hodgkinson closed her school. I was worried because there aren't many good places to study in San Diego. My mom wasn't sure what to do either, so she arranged for me to work with the men's class of the small company. This was the first time I noticed the difference between men's and women's classes. With no girls present, the class was devoted more to building strength. Instead of little stretches and waltz steps, we were given exercises where we

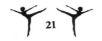

lifted our leg to hip level and held it there. My leg would start shaking, and I would be in absolute agony.

We would also have a marathon of jumping. The ballet master would tell us each to do one tour en l'air (a jump with a single turn before we land). Then he would ask us to do two turns, then three. I could never do three and I only did two well sometimes, and that was usually only to the right. Dancers soon discover they are right- or left-legged—like right- or left-handed—and everything works better on one side than the other. That's why we do everything in both directions. Otherwise, we would be unbalanced.

Since most of the men in the class were not very advanced, I didn't have much trouble keeping up. Everyone was nice to me, and I had some very challenging sessions. The biggest problem was that I was no longer studying the Royal Academy style. These new classes were combinations of whatever styles worked with the music.

After a year in the men's class, I worked once again with the company in the *Nutcracker*. I didn't bother with the larger company because of all the rehearsal conflicts. There had also been another problem—two of their three gingerbread casts got the chicken pox. Fortunately, I was not among them. The big company could have its large casts and endless rehearsals and chicken pox and everything. I was happy being Fritz again in the small company.

I then had the first of my own problems. Early in the fall I was injured doing a tourjeté (a turning leap where you jump from one foot to the other). It is a step that commonly causes injuries. The doctor said I had pulled the ligament that runs from the ankle

I had fun being Fritz again.

down the foot. It was extremely painful and did not seem to heal well. After two months, the doctor finally put my foot in a cast so I could not dance on it or move it the wrong way. I had the cast on for many of the *Nutcracker* rehearsals. That was pretty crazy now that I think back. I was worried about being replaced, but there was no one to take that part because I was the only boy they had.

At this time, dance and rehearsals took up most of my life. I didn't have many other activities outside of school except skateboarding with a few of my friends. The cast put a damper on that for a while too. I had a great skateboard and saved my allowance money for a set of ball-bearing wheels that cost $60. But with all my dancing, I never had time to learn the real fancy skateboarding stuff like jumping and crazy turning.

One of my few other interests was the Boy Scouts. My dad had been very active in it when he was young, and he got me involved in the local troop. During the summer I had one of the most exciting adventures when the troop went to Catalina Island for two weeks. It was the neatest camp I had ever seen. There was a rifle range, an archery range, and even a live buffalo walking around by the beach. We went on hikes and had swimming races, and it was a terrific two weeks for everyone. When we got back, we received jacket patches to go with the badges we had earned during the time at camp. I earned my swimming badge and an archery badge. I continued scouting activities throughout the year and attended the meetings that didn't interfere with dance rehearsals. They didn't have a badge for dance, but I earned one in theater arts.

In the spring of 1977, the ballet company had grown in size, quality, and reputation. They added a production of *Coppélia* to their program, and I was cast as the Chinaman in the second act. *Coppélia* is a ballet comedy with one of the usual silly storylines. This one is about a girl who pretends she is a doll to attract a man who is in love with a doll that was created by a man named Dr. Coppelius. The girl throws out the doll and takes its place. Then she tries to convince the doctor that he is a magician and brought her to life. The Chinaman is another doll in Dr. Coppelius's toy shop that does an exciting dance when it is wound up. This was the first time I really got to perform. There were so many leaps in my part that I sometimes got applause before I finished. The most exciting thing was being asked to sign autographs afterward. Little girls came up to me shyly holding out their programs.

That summer, the company began to fall apart and I discovered that Miss Hodgkinson was the new director of the San Diego Ballet School. I left the dying company and began classes once again with the English-style training. Unfortunately, I had so many bad habits that I didn't do too well. I was also still having problems with my feet.

The injury to my tendon had healed, but the difficulty seemed to be with the foot itself. It was almost flat, and the arch was not forming as it should for a dancer. This not only weakened my foot when I did a relevé (standing on half-toe), but it also made an ugly, unimpressive shape when I pointed my toe. Pointing the toe comes from the arch and not by curling the toes under as some beginners think.

Now that I was back with a group of girls close to my age, I had to prove myself all over again. I was the only boy in my class, and the girls were determined to make fun of me. One of them in particular went out of her way to criticize me. We soon developed a mutual

When I was on the football team at school, I never got to play because of dance injuries.

hatred. Oddly, later in the year she began to respect my abilities and even asked my advice occasionally. We later became good friends, and she even said she hoped someday I would partner her.

The following winter there was another *Nutcracker*, and an opportunity to dance at the Civic with the San Diego Ballet. My friend, Gabor, and I were the only two boys in a cast calling for eight boys. The other boys' roles were played by girls with wigs and boys' costumes. The entire cast of soldiers was girls too. That year, Mom had a semimajor role. It was fun being in the same ballets with her. Once we were cast as a mother and son at an audition, and they didn't know we really were mother and son.

My performances went well, but I did one really dumb thing. There was a girl in the performance whom I had known and worked with before. She was three years older than I and very pretty. I decided to try and win her attention by using my allowance money to buy her a dozen baby roses. I gave them to her just before the performance one night. She took the flowers, thanked me, and then never spoke to me except to try and make me feel like some stupid little kid. I was so embarrassed that it was a long time before I ever tried to give anyone flowers again.

The following February something happened that was the major turning point in my career. The San Diego School got notice that the School of American Ballet was having an audition in Los Angeles. This is the official school for the New York City Ballet, which is one of the greatest companies in the United States. If I got in, it would mean a chance to someday be a part of that company.

Mom did not want me to audition because she was not ready to move to New York, even for a summer

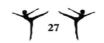

course. But I knew I had to go. So I did a sneaky thing. I asked Miss Hodgkinson to talk to her about it. Miss Hodgkinson thought the audition would be a good experience for me. I don't think she believed I would get in, and I think she said so to Mom because suddenly I was registered for the audition.

From what I could discover, notices for the auditions had been sent to all the major ballet schools in the country. Probably in Los Angeles alone, there would be several hundred dancers competing for a few openings. This would be the first time I would be seen by the big time, and I was determined to not only do my best but to get chosen. For over a month and a half I had New York on my brain. I worked my hardest. Every move in class was for a purpose. All the girls seemed to have the same idea, and we were the most serious ballet class anyone could have ever imagined. We worked and worked, and soon there was only one week left before the big moment.

A Westerner in the
East

The Los Angeles audition for the School of American Ballet was to be held in a studio in the middle of the city. The audition was what is known to most dancers as a "cattle call." This means everyone and his hamster shows up to try out. I arrived an hour early and was put with a more advanced group of fifty boys. If that was not enough to make me nervous, I was also the youngest and the smallest. I am not a fast grower, and most boys my age are taller. Even though I was eleven, I looked eight, which was both an advantage and a disadvantage. The advantage was that I looked cute and was seen more than the others. The disadvantage was that I was afraid I would not grow tall enough to be a dancer. Now that companies are hiring women five feet, seven inches and over, a man has to be at least six feet one to partner her. Although I was supposed to be twelve years old to audition, they let me try.

My insides were in knots, more so than anytime I was onstage. I felt like my whole life was at stake. The combinations were quick and confusing, and I was hidden behind the tall boys. It took everything I had to keep from crying, which would have been all I needed to be completely humiliated. Everything we did was difficult. Then we had to wait for our numbers to be called out. When mine was not one of them, I kept myself together long enough to get dressed and go out to Dad's car. Then I cried.

I didn't know what to think after that. Mom told me that I was probably too young to be seriously considered, but I secretly hoped that the School of American Ballet would accept me. Four weeks later a letter did arrive, but it stated that I did not make the summer course. It was worded, though, to make me think they might be interested in me for the future. I was especially encouraged when I found out that only one other student at San Diego Ballet got a letter like mine. Besides the two people who were accepted, the others didn't get anything. When I asked Mom to find out more about the letter, she agreed. But she also made it clear that she had no intention of living in New York. She had been there once before and hated it. I knew I would have a real fight to convince her otherwise.

The worst fights I had were in school. With my tight schedule, I was rarely available for a social life. When I couldn't go somewhere, I was told I was a snob. I had to get a special permission slip to get out of taking phys ed classes because I could train the wrong muscles or get injured. The snide remarks from the other boys grew worse. They were always asking me where I kept my tutu. They would go on and on, twirling around with their fingers on their heads and calling me a ballerina. Finally, one day, I hit someone. We got into a fistfight; he ended up with a broken hand and I ended up in the principal's office with a black eye.

Somehow through all that, I managed to get good grades. Most of my teachers liked me, but they told my mom that I was too much of a perfectionist. I would do the same assignment over and over until it was past due. That was one reason I got B+ grades instead of straight A's.

When I did have free time, I used to go with Dad to the bay, where he raced his sailboat. While he was out sailing, I rode my skateboard and hung around with other kids who were there. Once a bunch of us were running in the parking lot, and I tripped and hit my

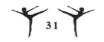

head on a boat trailer. My forehead was cut from one side to the other, and I had to get nineteen stitches. I was always doing weird things like that to myself.

The dumbest thing I ever did was a time at Dad's house when I was looking at a fillet knife he kept in his fishing box. Somehow I managed to cut open my finger and ended up with six stitches. The funny part of it was that several nights later there was a banquet for our Boy Scout troop and we got our badges. I was to be awarded my patch for safe knife and axe handling, and there I was accepting it with a big bandage on my finger!

Lots of interesting things happened to me that spring after the audition for SAB. The San Diego Ballet hired guest teachers to give master classes. Two of these teachers in particular had a big influence on me.

The first was a man from the Royal Academy in London named Alan Hooper. He taught two master classes, and from these classes he chose four finalists for a special scholarship. I figured if I could get a scholarship, I could convince Mom to try again to get me into the School of American Ballet and reconsider moving to New York. I knew she was tired of San Diego and was looking for possible places to move to. I had to convince her to move East.

The class with Mr. Hooper was incredible. He really liked me too. When Miss Hodgkinson posted the list of finalists, I was on it with three girls. Even though I had studied some men's technique in the past, Mr. Hooper saw that I needed extra work for strength, and he took extra time to show me how to better use my muscles for jumps. I realized more than ever how much I needed that kind of training. Girls' classes were all right to get me dancing, but I needed something more to build strength. Even Miss Hodgkinson admitted that I should go somewhere else soon to get the training I needed.

What I wanted most was to be in a class of boys my own age, taught by a man who had once been a principal dancer himself. This desire pushed me into signing up for a master class with Sean Greene. The San Diego Ballet hosted a performance of the Bella Lewitzky modern dance company, and Sean was one of their principals. I had never had a modern class in my life, but I figured it was all dance and I could dance, so it couldn't be that complicated. Was I in for a surprise! I showed up dressed for Royal Academy–style class in black tights and a white T-shirt. Everyone else was in odd, assorted colors and bare feet. The shoes and socks came off, and someone cut the feet off my tights. Several people looked at me oddly, and I felt very out of place.

All the modern students were more experienced than I. Most of them were at least six years older too. Some of the other Lewitzky company members would help me with a position. We did not have a barre session; we began working on the floor. I knew nothing about arching and contracting my back and stomach. It was like I was dancing with people from outer space.

When we began to move across the floor, everything changed for me. The group not only had an accompanist on the piano, but a flute player too. The music was so beautiful and inspiring that my body began to move even though it wanted to do ballet. Soon I was doing huge leaps and turns across the studio and surprising everyone there—including myself. The ex-

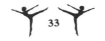

perience didn't make me want to run out and join a modern dance school, but it made me see that other dance forms were important too. When the dancers from Bella Lewitzky heard this was my first modern class, they told me to come back and see them in a few years if I wanted a job. This was the first time I saw an alternative to classical ballet, but it would be several years before I thought about it seriously.

The scholarship selection by Alan Hooper put me into a new project. David was one of the company men assigned to work with me in a piece of choreography that I was to perform before a group of judges. After the *Nutcracker* the previous winter, David had not been too fond of me. Gabor and I had shared a dressing room with him and three others, and we had not been very well behaved. But as David and I worked on the audition dance, we began to respect each other. The music he chose was wonderful. It was Tchaikovsky's Suite in G, which is the music used for a ballet called *Theme and Variations*. We didn't use the entire piece, just one of the more exciting parts. My dance was mostly mime. I was supposed to be a paperboy trying to sell unwanted papers. Suddenly someone buys them all, and I am so happy that I do a joyful dance with leaps and turns.

The four of us competed for two scholarships by performing in a local meeting-hall auditorium. The floor of the stage was like an ice rink and a quarter of it was taken up by a piano. The three girls were terrified of slipping in their pointe shoes. One of them did fall during her dance, but was unhurt. I ended up in a long slide, but I somehow managed to stay upright. The idea of using the scholarship as a way to get Mom to New York began to seem less and less likely, especially when I didn't succeed. The judges thought I was cute, but they gave the awards to the more advanced students.

I didn't have time to think about being disappointed. Soon after the competition, I began rehearsals for the school production of *The Emperor's Nightingale.* This is a Chinese fairy tale about a nightingale that is captured by an emperor. Its singing is so beautiful that it cures his illness, and he lets it go. There are lots of other characters involved, including a frog. I was cast as the frog, a solo role that involved some of the best music in the ballet and lots of jumping.

The costumes were terrific. They were designed by a costumer from London's Royal Ballet. I wore a green leotard and tights and a Chinese dragonlike frog head. The problem was that every time I did a turn, I was uncertain which direction I would be facing when I landed. The head would twist and I couldn't spot (this is finding a point to focus on and whipping your head around to that point to keep from getting dizzy). During the performance I was lucky to land facing front each time. The little kids in the audience were very funny. After the bows they stormed backstage to see what the frog looked like.

This was the first time my dad really saw me dance. He came up to me later and congratulated me on a nice job. I could tell he was proud.

Lots of things began to happen very quickly then. The San Diego Ballet began to have many problems. I got out the letter that the School of American Ballet had sent me and reread it. Then I got up my courage and asked Mom once again if she could call the school about the winter session. By this time, she had already tried to sell me on every school in the United States that was not in New York. She had even suggested Europe. But she admitted later that she knew New York was the only place that made sense.

The School of American Ballet said I could re-audition. A week later, we were on our way to the Big Apple.

We were able to stay with two girls from the San Diego Ballet School who were in the SAB summer program. I had heard all kinds of horror stories about New York City and was not sure what to expect. I figured we might get mugged the minute we stepped off the plane, but the place actually looked very civilized.

The first day there we explored Lincoln Center and several of the schools, including School of American Ballet and American Ballet Theatre School. My audition was scheduled to take place the next day. That evening we went to a production of the Joffrey Ballet. I finally got to see Nureyev dance in person.

My audition was at noon the next day. The studios were the best I have ever seen; each one was twice the size of the largest studio in the San Diego Ballet and had a triple row of barres. I changed into my ballet clothes and felt almost sick to my stomach as we waited to be called in. We waited and waited, but no one called us. Finally, Mom stuck her head inside the director's office and asked if she was running late. It turned out that the temporary receptionist had not even told the director we were there, so I was going to get a special audition.

I was terrified. There I was with one Russian lady walking in front of me and another in back. I felt like I was on my way to an execution instead of an audition.

The first day we were in New York we explored Lincoln Center.

They weren't mean or anything, but I knew this was probably my last big chance. If I blew this audition, I would probably have to quit dance.

Because we missed the regular audition time, there wasn't a free studio anywhere. I ended up holding onto the drinking fountain in the hall and using it for a barre. They had me do a tendue (stretching of my foot) to the front, side, and back and then one of the women picked up my leg to see how limber I was. I was never very limber, and my leg wouldn't go any higher than hip level. Also my dumb feet still didn't point worth anything. The women kept talking in Russian, but I got the idea that they liked my body. They especially liked my triple pirouette (turn) to the right.

I was taken back to the reception area, and the director asked to speak with my mother. I sat in the hall. Even my temples pounded from my fast heartbeat. Whatever Mom told me in the next few minutes was going to affect the rest of my life.

The next thing I knew I was looking up at Mom. Her look caught mine and she smiled. I thought I was going to faint from relief. She didn't even have to tell me I was in. We went out to lunch to celebrate my good fortune.

Mom was happy for me; she also realized she would have to move to New York by September so I could attend the school. We had two days to find an apartment, something that is next to impossible in that city. But we were lucky. We found a small, one-bedroom apartment close to Lincoln Center in a building that was being renovated.

Not only was the move itself a tremendous project, but we had barely a month and a half to find good tenants for our house in San Diego and a place to store most of our furniture. Mom typed up a resumé and sent it to all the major New York ballet schools to apply for a job as an administrator.

We were nervous wrecks for the next two months. As Mom was finishing her job with the San Diego Ballet, one of the other dancers pulled her aside and suggested she have a long facts-of-life talk with me about homosexuals. Mom and I had discussed the subject before, but never in any kind of detail. I knew that homosexuals were interested in others of their own sex, but I had no idea what they did or how I could be approached by one of them. Mom basically wanted to warn me not to get myself into any situation where I could be approached.

Somehow a miracle happened. Everything began to work out. The house was rented, the animals had homes, and the extra furniture was put into storage. All of us were exhausted from cleaning and packing. We had decided to drive a scenic route to the East, going through Arizona, New Mexico, Texas, Oklahoma, Missouri, Illinois, Indiana, Ohio, West Virginia, Pennsylvania, and New Jersey. We were taking all our belongings in a trailer, the least expensive way to move. I was excited about the trip, but most excited about my new life as a ballet dancer on scholarship at one of the best schools in the world.

Even though Stephanie and I both had been all over the world, we were fascinated by our trip across the United States. All the way to New York we badgered Mom to stop and let us see all kinds of things. We visited the Painted Desert and the Petrified Forest, and along the way we stopped at the phony trading posts, where we bought lots of Indian jewelry and a Navaho rug.

We generally had a wonderful time, but it seemed that the farther east we drove, the more tension we felt. By the time we reached the Pennsylvania Turnpike, Mom was in a terrible mood. When I gave her the wrong directions, she almost snapped my head off. I think she was nervous because somehow she suspected the mess we were to find when we arrived in New York City.

In Pennsylvania, we stopped and Mom put in a second call to the realtor of the apartment building. We had called before we left California to be certain the construction was completed and we would be able to move in. At that time we were told the building was beautiful and the apartment was ready and waiting. We all had the idea we would be moved in and completely settled before I began classes the following Monday. We had even planned to sightsee that weekend with a trip to the Statue of Liberty.

When we got into Manhattan, the realtor asked us what we were doing there. After parking the trailer outside the building, we stepped over dirt piles in the lobby and realized someone had really put one over on us. We were allowed to store our belongings in the apartment. Then Mom had to sign a release that said the landlord was not responsible for any of our things. I couldn't believe how small the place was. After a three-story house, this one-bedroom apartment was like a closet. I tried to lighten things up by pointing to a mouse and saying I thought we weren't allowed to have pets.

With very little money left, we drove to New Jersey to find an inexpensive place to stay. As soon as we headed west, we were tempted to keep going and not stop.

The one bright spot was going to the School of American Ballet to tell them I was in the city. Because the new term hadn't started yet, the school was unusually quiet and beautiful—almost like a movie set. I saw my teacher, Jean-Pierre Bónnefous, but couldn't meet him as he was in a hurry to leave. I was really looking forward to taking classes with such a famous man. He was not only a principal dancer with the New York City Ballet but was also from the Paris Opera Company.

The other nice thing that happened was that Mom was offered a job as an administrative assistant at the school. We would be at the same ballet studio again, but this time it would be the best. We had our lives partially organized in New York City, but had no place to live.

Our next problem was finding an academic school. Until now, none of us gave it too much thought. Mom figured it would be just like in California—we would enroll in the neighborhood school. The neighborhood school was an experience all its own. As we walked to the entrance, two kids in leather jackets moved out of our way. They had some kind of tire chains in their hands. The people inside the building weren't much better. Even the teachers looked tough. The lady at the desk wanted to see our immunization records, which Mom didn't have. The woman treated us quite rudely. We didn't want to go that that school anyway, and Mom was determined that we wouldn't. She found a phone book and called the Episcopalian church to ask about a private school. They told her about the Cathedral School of St. John the Divine and gave her the number. The place was unbelievable. The cathedral is one of the biggest in the world, and the school is next to it, a big stone-and-wood building that even had peacocks walking around on the lawn!

It was perfect, and Stephanie and I decided it was where we wanted to go. There was only one problem. Since it was a private school, it cost a fortune. In fact, Mom said it would cost more than one month's salary for one of us to go there. We were really disappointed.

When we went to talk to the headmaster, Mom asked what we could do. I think at the time she would have kept us out of school completely rather than have us go to that public school.

The headmaster said they might be able to help us with a scholarship but we had to have excellent grades and do well on a particular test. Luckily, Stephanie and I had both been good students. Even better, the exams we were to take were the same ones we had taken at our school in San Diego three months before to check on our progress.

I remembered everything and had no trouble getting through the test. Stephanie and I both were done early. We handed in the exams, and the headmaster

I knew I wanted to go to Cathedral School the first time I saw it.

Boys had to wear a blazer and tie at Cathedral School.

told Mom to call the school later that afternoon for the results. We walked around the grounds some more and watched the peacocks and the squirrels. We also visited the cathedral, which was one of the most beautiful churches I had ever seen. The ceiling went up for miles and everything was carved, even the stones looked like lace. And everywhere you looked were stained-glass windows. It was hard to believe we were still in New York in the middle of Manhattan. Later that day, when Mom called the school, we found out that we both had won scholarships. We would start classes the next Monday. That evening we went shopping for school uniforms.

After the bush shorts and flowered shirts we wore to school in California, I had some trouble relating to

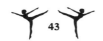

a blazer, slacks, a white shirt, and tie. Stephanie had her own problems having to wear a skirt. The East was really a whole new world to us. The only real problem I saw with the new school was the subjects. I was put into a second-year Latin class and a second-year French class, which would have been all right except that I had never had a foreign language, except for learning the French ballet terms. I had to be in second-year everything because I wouldn't be able to graduate without them.

We commuted into the city from the motel in central New Jersey and began our new life. At Cathedral School we only had seven students in a class. We had a different teacher for each subject and a homeroom. I was checked out as the new kid from California and by the end of the school day I must have heard every California joke invented. I left school with a ton of homework and went to the Juilliard School for my first ballet class at SAB.

I wore the same ballet uniform as I had for the Royal Academy classes: a white T-shirt, black tights, white socks, and black shoes. I had hoped to at least be able to wear white shoes and even had a new pair, but the uniform was black.

There were nine boys in my class and we were all within a year of each other in age. Most of them had been in last year's group, and when I arrived they stayed in one area of the studio and stared at me. But they were fairly friendly, except one. He was older than the others and also more advanced. He didn't like me at all. His favorite thing was to slam my head against a locker door. Two of the other boys who made friends with me said he used to get after them too when there were new. They suggested I take karate lessons.

The ballet class itself was terrific, especially Jean-Pierre. He was a patient man who never once yelled even when we did everything wrong. The big drawback was that he often went on tour. Then we were put in another class with a large group of girls who considered us intruders.

Between my dance classes, my schoolwork, and living in a motel, I was having a lot of troubles. Once we tried moving into a cheap hotel in the city, but that was a nightmare. When we went to check in, someone broke into the car and stole two of our suitcases. One of them had all my favorite clothes and my souvenirs from the trip. I couldn't believe it. No one ever did that to us before. It was an awful feeling. They even took my "I love New York" T-shirt. At that point, I

There were nine boys in my class at School of American Ballet.

almost hated New York. I saw a movie once called *The Out of Towners*. For a while, I wondered if we were making our own version.

The hotel room was another experience I would like to forget. A neon light outside lit up the room, and we could see the shadows of hundreds of cockroaches as they crawled on the walls and ceiling. We didn't even wait until morning to leave. We drove back to the motel in New Jersey and stayed there for over a month.

When we finally moved into the New York apartment, there was no water or electricity. Most of the other tenants were Juilliard students and dancers from various major companies. We all got together and had a rent strike. I'm sure it was very frustrating for Mom, but I kind of found it exciting. We had long extension cords running up and down the uncarpeted halls to plug in to the workman's electricity. When the fuses blew, people would wander all over the dark halls with candles. It was really weird, kind of like being in a haunted house or at a late-night monster movie.

At least I had an easier time now getting to and from my ballet classes, even though much of the time I was totally exhausted and had headaches from trying to do homework in the dim light of one lamp. I also kept getting sick because we had no heat.

Two friends of my Mom's from the San Diego Ballet called and asked if we could put them up until they found an apartment in the city. Mom said the place was like a community artists' tenement anyway, so why not?

The good usually followed the bad, and I was about to have my first big break as a dancer in New York

City. Word was out that I was being considered for the role of prince in the famous New York City Ballet *Nutcracker.* It was the kind of role some kids would do almost anything to get. It was one of the few principal roles a child could have in the adult ballet world. Every male student five feet and under tried out for it. The major New York City news stations taped portions of the auditions for the evening news, and over a hundred anxious parents stood waiting in the Juilliard halls. I was featured on the news, but I didn't get the part. I was already five feet tall and they figured I would grow. Since the boy they choose has the role for two years, they were afraid I would be too tall the following year and wouldn't fit into the costume. I was finally cast as one of the boys in the party scene— not my favorite part — but it was a great chance to work with the New York City Ballet and see George Balanchine.

What was really crazy that morning of the audition was the way the other kids' parents reacted. As the students came out of the studios, some were crying and some were skipping down the corridor with the mimeographed schedules they gave the new cast members. One little girl told her mother she didn't get a role, and I couldn't believe it when the girl's mother burst into tears. My friend John came out and jumped into the air. He had been chosen as the prince. I handed my schedule to Mom and wished like crazy it had been me.

By the end of October the weather had turned unbelievably cold. Since it rarely got below freezing in California, I was not used to the bitter Manhattan wind. We still had no electricity, heat, or hot water in the apartment. Ice-water showers were the only way to get clean. The two friends from San Diego were staying with us, and we spent many evenings huddled around one lamp eating pizza. This was not the vision I had of fancy New York City living. The apartment was so cold we were wearing dancer's warmups day and night. I was beginning to welcome classes and rehearsals just to be in a warm building.

The one thing I found to be the most interesting in my life was seeing and meeting so many famous people. Jerome Robbins was often in Mom's office, as were Peter Martins and Suzanne Farrell. Sometimes I had a glimpse of Mikhail Baryshnikov, who was still with City Ballet at that time.

While rehearsing the *Nutcracker*, I discovered that the company member who played my stage father was a neighbor in the same awful building we lived in. I was not a groupie type and was not overly impressed by celebrities, but I had to admit I had an unusual opportunity. And I was definitely in awe of Mr. Balanchine. To me, he was like the father of ballet.

Mom was able to get tickets for the opening night gala performance of the City Ballet. I was going to see the company live onstage for the first time. Seeing them live instead of on TV or in rehearsal was terrific. They premiered a new piece by Peter Martins. I never saw so many long-legged ballerinas in my life.

The weird part of the gala was the intermission. I hadn't eaten since lunchtime, and I tried to get a sandwich from the buffet table. All these fat women in mink coats kept stepping on my feet and elbowing me out of the way.

When I finally got a sandwich and was standing in the lobby eating, an elderly man came up to me and remarked that I had to be a dancer. He looked like he had been a famous dancer himself once. Mom didn't recognize him but agreed. The man wished me good luck with my career and I felt like it was a good sign for my future.

By the end of November, we had lights and hot water. It was almost livable. I was trying to balance rehearsals with homework, and even though I was always a fairly good student, I was failing Latin. The pressure to do homework and take ballet class and

At first, I had trouble keeping up with the schoolwork.

rehearse until eleven at night was terrible. I tried to study in the backstage lounge area at the State Theatre, but people wandered by and constantly talked to me. We were going to have twenty performances of the *Nutcracker,* including a gala benefit where I had to appear afterward in costume and sign autographs for the children who attended the matinee.

Even though I was in one of the large theaters in Lincoln Center, it was difficult for me to realize where I actually was. From the stage area, the theater did not look much larger than the San Diego Civic. Once the stage lights were on and we couldn't see the audience, it was really little different. The spectacular part of it all was being with the New York City Ballet and knowing I was in New York City at last. In California, I had always worn a sweatshirt that said, "Property of New York City Ballet." I never truly believed that they would ever pay me to perform with them.

The day of the big gala was my worst. I woke up that morning with food poisoning. Mom tried to contact someone to have me replaced, but couldn't reach anyone. We didn't know what to do, so I took a large dose of antacid and waited. I still felt terrible but was not sick to my stomach, so we went to the theater. Mom went with me and made arrangements to be in the wings backstage in case I had to be taken offstage quickly. It was a real tense situation. In the dressing room mirror, I looked absolutely white, even with stage makeup. They tried to put color on my cheeks and it showed up like round clown spots. My dance was fairly complicated, but I somehow managed to get through it without looking too ill. The only time I thought I wasn't going to make it was when we all sat by the Christmas tree watching the soldier doll dance. I was never so glad in my life as when that party scene ended. In fact, I felt so good afterward that I was able to go out and sign autographs.

As if I didn't have enough to do with ballet, I became involved in a theater production at Cathedral School. They did original musicals that were written by my English teacher. The music was done by the choir director of the cathedral. Because of my crazy schedule, I only tried out for a small part. Mom thought it was important for me to have experience in acting and singing in case my dancing didn't work out. She never really wanted me to be a dancer because she knew what a hard life it is. But she wanted me to be happy, so she agreed to support whatever I chose to do. I had no intention of becoming an actor then. Doing the plays was a favor to her.

Soon after the *Nutcracker*, I began to have more problems with my feet. Both my heels hurt just to stand on them, let alone dance. The company doctor took X-rays and discovered that I had bruised the heel bones. He said I would have to stop dancing for three months. He also said that if the bones didn't heal well, I might have to stop dancing completely. For a while I was on crutches and wore thick pads in the heels of both shoes. It was so boring to have to just sit and watch classes all the time. I wanted to be dancing and was afraid I would lose my scholarship if I wasn't back soon. Mom gave me good advice during that time. She said as long as I couldn't dance, I should

When I was injured, it was boring having to just sit and watch the class.

work on my stretching and get more limber. I was always tight and could rarely get all the way down into the splits. It seemed whenever I just about made it into a full split, I would begin to grow and my tendons would get shorter.

By April, I was much more limber and back in class, but my dancing wasn't so terrific because I was weak and out of practice. It seemed as though I was so far behind in my technique that I would probably be held back another year in the same class. Mom bought me a pair of pointe shoes to try and strengthen my feet and ankles. I kept them a deep dark secret from my nondance friends and only practiced with them at home. Going up on the toes will develop strength faster than other ways of working the feet. I used the window sill for a barre and spent fifteen

I even stretched while I did homework.

minutes a day going up and down on my toes. I also hoped the exercises would help develop my arches better. One thing I could do that pleased me was that I could extend my leg above hip level.

Late that month I had my worst experience in New York. I was mugged.

I was working on a special report on Ireland for my social studies class and I went to a local bookstore for a book on Yeats. On the way back, on the corner in front of my own building, a boy about three years older than I grabbed me around the neck. There was another boy who looked younger and a third who was about my age. They demanded my money. I took out my wallet, and my hand shook so badly I could hardly get out my change from the five dollars I had used for the book. I even offered them my bus pass, but they gave it back. They said they wouldn't hurt me, but it didn't make me less scared. When I got home, I could barely tell Mom about it.

For a long time afterward, I was edgy whenever I saw a group of boys standing around in front of a building. I would walk way out of my way to avoid them. I also began to carry money in my shoe if I had over five dollars.

Luckily, my busy schedule did not allow me much time to think about this. I was not only cast in another school musical but was also a member of the school rocket club. I spent three months building and painting a fancy model rocket, and that spring the club went to a park in the Bronx to launch our masterpieces. I traded my engine for a stronger one, thinking I would give the rocket a super flight. I lit the thing and it blasted up into the air and up and up and then it shot over a grove of trees and disappeared forever. I tried building a second rocket, but never had the opportunity to try it out.

The school play was a big success. It was a takeoff on *Macbeth*, a modern musical version. I had another small role but had lots of fun doing it.

About this same time, an eight-page cover story was published about me in *Youth Magazine*. It was weird how that came about. We met the author on our trip across the United States when we stopped in Phoenix. It was really hot, so we ran out and jumped in the pool. This nice man was there who said he was a writer from New York and was interested in us because we were going there to live. When I told him I was going there on scholarship with the School of American Ballet, he became even more interested. He said he had a son who danced and he wanted to know all about the school. Then he gave us his phone number and told us to call him later in the month, that he was interested in doing a story on me. I never thought I would be on the front and back cover. I think the story helped my career a little too.

By June, I was evaluated at the School of American Ballet. The word was that I was doing fine but I would definitely remain in the lower-level class. My disappointment was slightly less when a representative from the Berlin Opera Ballet came to SAB. Several of us were invited to work with Nureyev and Valery Panov in their production of the *Nutcracker*. We were to begin rehearsals after the July Fourth weekend.

I had also completed my first academic year at Cathedral School, where I got A and B grades in ev-

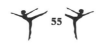

Here I'm being evaluated at School of American Ballet.

erything, including Latin and French. Around the middle of the year, those subjects became clearer to me, but not without a lot of extra work. And I have to admit, they were never my favorites.

At the beginning of rehearsals for the Berlin Opera, I learned I was cast once again in the *Nutcracker* party scene, but I got to do more. Nureyev's production is different from the usual ones because it begins and ends with the party scene. Also, I was a soldier this time. Nureyev rehearsed us some of the time. He was always dressed in leather and seemed to have a very short temper. He was always nice to me, but I wasn't sure how to take him. We spent what seemed like hours going over and over the same ballet scene as soldiers fighting the mice.

I soon discovered I was also cast in a second production. I came home and told Mom I was in some stupid thing called *The Idiot.* I had no idea what a classic it was. But Mom had already heard the ballet was to be a United States premiere. It was based on a book by a famous Russian author named Dostoevski. Not only was Nureyev going to star in it, but also Valery and Galina Panov, two other famous Russian ballet stars.

We danced with the little girls who were given the opportunity to be on their toes. One of them got to do a short duet with Nureyev. This was also my first time onstage at the Metropolitan Opera House. The Met was similar to the State Theatre in that once we were onstage with the lights dimmed, it could have been anywhere. But I knew this was special. This was the stage everyone in California dreamed of seeing from the curtain side.

I was dressed as a young Russian cadet and had this crazy tall hat that I was constantly afraid of losing. We also got to take bows at the end of the performance.

It was unreal being on that stage with these legendary dancers, hearing bravos echoing all around us. Suddenly all the trouble and worries in New York were worth it. This was why we had come here. This was what it was all about. And it was just beginning for me.

The Graduate

I spent half the summer flying back and forth from my dad's place in Minnesota to New York City. First, I made a brief visit between the Berlin Opera Ballet performances. The reason for my next trip was even more exciting.

When Cathedral School had its musical production *Macbeth*, I was given a wonderful new opportunity. Evidently, talent scouts had been all over the city checking out drama schools for a boy with a particular look to star in a new movie. I received a mimeographed letter stating I should go see a casting director sometime in July. Mom made an appointment for me, and I flew back once again from Minnesota.

The office was in a fancy building near Times Square. Several other boys waited in the reception area; all of us were blue-eyed blonds. Each of us was given several pages of a script to study, so there wasn't much conversation.

In the director's office, I was looked over by several people while a very nice lady talked to me about my career plans. Then I was asked to read my section of the script. Since I had little acting training at the time, my presentation was not too terrific, but they seemed to like me anyway. I didn't get the part and wasn't too disappointed until the movie came out. It was a major award winner called *On Golden Pond*.

I didn't know at the time that the movie was to star Katharine Hepburn. She is one of my favorite actresses. The first time I saw her was in a movie we watched on TV one afternoon, called *The African Queen*. It was one of the best movies I've ever seen. I also really liked *On Golden Pond* and wished that I could have had the role of the little boy. But the boy who got the part was a much better actor than I was.

Also, I had braces on my teeth and I think that eliminated me too.

I had one big worry that was always with me. What if I didn't succeed as a dancer? What would I do? In school, I seemed to be particularly good at math and I was interested in computers. But computers and dancing are not exactly compatible. I was also beginning to see more opportunities in acting and I had a job with the New York City Opera in their production of *The Merry Wives of Windsor*. One of the advantages of going to school at the School of American Ballet was that every time another company needed children for a production they came to us. This time not only would I be performing at Lincoln Center but I was going on tour with the opera company to Los Angeles to perform at the Dorothy Chandler Pavilion.

I had a lot to do when I returned that fall from Minnesota to begin my senior year at Cathedral School. I was also expected to make a choice of where I would go to high school. In the West, we just went to the local one. But here in New York, everything was a choice. With my performing life-style, I had only two choices. The first was Performing Arts High School, which was close to impossible to get into after the screening of the movie *Fame*. The second was Professional Children's School, a school designed to work around the schedules of performers in both dance and theater. I applied to both.

Performing Arts High School required an audition. Jean-Pierre Bonnefous agreed to choreograph a dance for me for the audition. We listened to lots of different music and finally decided on a small two-minute part from *Billy the Kid*. Jean-Pierre and I experimented with different kinds of steps. Some of them were from

Jean Pierre agreed to help me with my audition piece.

the original ballet and others were too difficult for me. We decided to highlight my jumping ability, so he made up lots of impressive leaps. I'll never forget how wonderful he was, taking his own time to work with me and rehearse me until I had the dance perfected.

The audition itself was like the scene in *Fame* except with several hundred more people. The day I went was not the only day they saw dancers. It's hard to say just how many people were involved. All the kids auditioning waited in a very cold common area that I think was the cafeteria. We stood around bundled to the ears in our winter coats, waiting to be called. Each department delegated students to certain areas of the room, so all the dancers were grouped together, the actors were across the room, and the musicians were next to the actors. Some kids were doing last-minute memorizing of scripts, others were stretching cold muscles, and others were hugging large instrument cases and displaying terrified expressions. Tension was high.

The dancers were taken ten at a time. We went upstairs to a studio and changed into dance clothes. I made friends with two other boys. One of them said this was the only school he had applied to. I thought he was taking a big chance. I felt kind of sorry for him, wondering what he'd do if he didn't get in (but he did).

We did our dances for the judges. Actually we only did part of our dances because there were so many people auditioning. Three of us were given call-back sheets: I, the boy I spoke with, and the other boy I met. I had mixed feelings. Even though Performing Arts High School was free, it did not allow for a performing schedule outside its curriculum. But Professional Children's School was expensive. I would have to make a difficult choice if I was accepted by both schools.

In the meantime, rehearsals began for the opera. This was a whole different world from ballet, even

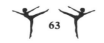

though I was hired as a ballet dancer. We got to meet Beverly Sills and she is a very nice lady. One night she signed my program. Most of the other artists were nice to us also. I had the role of one of Falstaff's followers. Falstaff is the lead character in the opera, an old man whom everyone, including us, eventually makes into a complete fool. I will say the singer who played Falstaff was definitely not a fool. He was a very talented actor and singer.

I had always hated opera. It made me think of a fat lady with braids and a spear, singing with a voice that would break mirrors. Mom took Stephanie and me to see *Carmen* once, and we fidgeted and fought so much that she swore she would never take us to an opera again.

But working with City Opera changed all that. Being behind the scenes at the opera made it all much more real to me. These people trained their voices as hard as dancers trained their muscles, and they were every bit as dedicated.

We went to California in November. I was excited about performing at the Dorothy Chandler Pavilion, because I had thought it was the greatest theater in the world when I was eight. Then I wasn't familiar with the Met. Performing in the Dorothy Chandler was like living out a childhood dream.

Another thing that pleased me about dancing in Los Angeles was that Nana, my mother's mother, was going to see me perform. She had seen me in the *Nutcracker* and followed my career, but I felt that she thought I wasn't really serious about dance. When she saw me in the opera I knew she was very proud. She came backstage and treated me like I was the star of the show. I felt very special.

Mom was my biggest fan when I performed in New York.

There aren't too many moments when a performer is aware of the audience as individuals, even when members of the family are there. Each performance gets to be like the others. Then someone special will come backstage like Nana did that night and everything changes. I guess that's what performing is all about.

In Los Angeles, the opera company let us go sightseeing. The Disneyland tour was the most fun. I had been there many times but I still loved it. There was always something new to see, some new ride or exhibit.

Another thing I got to do was play video games. We were paid fifteen dollars a day spending money, and I don't know how many quarters I plugged into those machines. At the time, the most popular game was Asteroids. I would play game after game trying to get the highest score. Usually, I would be number six or something, but at least I would get my initials on the screen. There was a video machine in the restaurant of our hotel, and I spent every spare minute I could playing it. It was a way to make all my worries and anger at people go away. I guess I was worried about a lot of things and angry at a lot of people, or something. Being a kid was hard sometimes.

The one thing none of us liked about the tour was the tutored homework sessions. The teachers at Cathedral School were not used to students going on the road. I had to make up my homework assignments in advance. The tutor we had in Los Angeles made us feel like we were two-year-olds with a babysitter. I don't think she liked being there any more than we liked having her. We really were awfully mean to her when I think back on it now. She must have thought we were a bunch of little creeps. One night we *were* a bunch of little creeps. The last night of performance we escaped from our chaperone and went to a nearby liquor store. We found these two mean-looking guys and asked them if they would buy us a bottle of wine. They bought us two bottles of cheap wine, one red and one white, and another bottle of fancy wine for themselves, which they bought with our money. We were afraid to say anything because we were breaking the law, and they didn't look like the kind of guys to challenge. We snuck the wine back to the hotel room and stayed up all night drinking. I had the worst headache of my life the next morning. When I told my mom later, she just said she was glad I was honest about it and half-smiled when she asked how I felt the next day.

I had not only a headache the next day but also one of the scariest experiences of my life. We were flying back to New York, and somewhere over the Midwest the airplane hit an air pocket and fell over 100 feet straight down. I was playing cards with two of my friends and our cards and our sodas went all over the place. Some woman a few rows ahead of us started yelling, "We're going down! We're going down! We'll all be killed!" Someone slapped her just like in those airplane disaster movies.

Only one person was hurt. A flight attendant had a food cart fall on her and I think her ankle was broken. The people in first class had been eating dinner and most of them ended up wearing their meals. I was fighting hard not to get sick to my stomach. One of my friends did get sick. I didn't realize how shaken up

I was until we landed. Mom was there to meet me at the airport and said I was a light green color. Someone told her to get me a cup of tea because I was in shock. I don't think my stomach felt normal until we got home.

After the tour to California, the School of American Ballet began rehearsals for the *Nutcracker* again. I didn't even audition because I was five foot one and you had to be five feet or under. I was also upset because I wasn't growing fast enough. Being too short could put me at a real disadvantage when I got older. Girls are at least four inches taller on toe, and small men have to work with tiny girls to look balanced. Most of the big companies are favoring long-legged, taller girls. But it's also a problem if boys grow too fast. Four to six inches of sudden growth can cause tendons to shorten and limberness to disappear, and that can make it difficult to jump or turn. At that time, boys also lose much of their strength and have problems with lifts, especially the press lifts where the girl is held over the boy's head like a barbell. Lifting a girl the wrong way can cause serious back problems. So, to say the least, I was getting very anxious. I kept thinking, what if I stay small? I could do everything perfectly and all my work would come to nothing. To add to my anxiety, my sister Stephanie was already five inches taller than I and everyone asked if I was her younger brother. I hated being small and I also hated being in the same school with her.

The teachers and staff at Cathedral were really supportive of my career. Some of them even came to my performances at Lincoln Center. The problem was with some of the other students. Several boys liked to prance around asking if I wore a tutu. One of them called me faggot. I couldn't wait until I graduated and went someplace where everyone else was in the arts. Except for my friends at SAB and a couple of boys at Cathedral, I didn't have very many friends then. I pretended it didn't matter, but it did, especially on weekends when I had nothing to do and was afraid to go anywhere because I might get mugged. My height didn't help me look very tough, and I was

I kept thinking, "What if I don't grow tall enough?"

contantly crossing the street to avoid any group of boys standing around.

Since I wasn't going to be in the *Nutcracker,* our family had one of our first real Christmases in a long time. We didn't even go to see a performance. One evening, we went down Broadway and bought a big tree, which was being sold in a makeshift lot outside a vegetable market. Stephanie, Mom, and I carried it home. After we got it in a stand, we went back out and bought lots of groceries like soda and chips and dip mixes and then invited over the scholarship students from American Ballet Theatre, where Mom now had a

The mirrors in the studio would get smeared from heat and perspiration.

job. We decided to have our first annual tree-trimming party.

The party was lots of fun. We paraded around wearing some of the decorations and played games and laughed a lot. After all the clowning, we actually decorated the tree. It looked great. I was also able to compare notes with many of the Ballet Theatre kids and realized how many of them had begun training at SAB. We all seemed to be on the same course: the local hometown school to SAB and then on to the New York City Ballet, Ballet Theatre, or the Joffrey.

Stephanie and I spent New Year's Eve with our dad in Minnesota and Mom went to California. When we returned to New York, I was cast in a new opera. It was a brand-new production called *The Cunning Little Vixen,* and all the characters were animals. Because I could jump, I was cast as the hawk, a role that required jumping from branches to rocks to other rocks to branches. The costumes were incredible; some of them cost as much as $5,000 apiece. I had to go to a loft apartment near Canal Street for fittings in the evening.

The costume loft was crazy. Huge pieces of Styrofoam and big bolts of fake fur were everywhere. My costume was made of Styrofoam, with a silky material covering the wings. At first the wings were designed so I could control some of the long feathers, but it was so complicated for me to operate that they made the feathers immobile. And you should have seen my feet! They were these crazy things with big claw toes attached to some kind of soft jazz shoes. I wore a yellow leotard and tights underneath. The foam was terribly hot, especially the hawk head. I had to look out from under the beak.

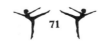

All the children—including the singing children—had to not only try on their costumes but move around in them. One afternoon the loft housed a jumping grasshopper, a crawling caterpillar, a waddling racoon, and me flapping and jumping around in my hawk costume. It looked like some kind of strange zoo. One of my good friends was the weasel, and he found his costume almost suffocating under the stage lights.

The opera received mixed reviews. But one thing everyone agreed about was the costumes. All the writers thought the costumes were sensational. *Vixen* was also scheduled to go to California the following fall. One night one of the producers gave each of us an autographed poster. It is still one of my treasures, along with a poster autographed by Peter Martins and Suzanne Farrell and a picture of me with Nureyev and the Panovs—me with my arm around beautiful Galina Panov.

With the money I saved from the opera salary, I decided to buy my own video game. I had been play-

Alex and I both were cast in *The Cunning Little Vixen.*

ing Asteroids at a place near our apartment, but I still didn't like wandering around on my own. One night a friend and I went over there and when we ran out of quarters, we went into the restaurant and sold people our subway tokens for more quarters.

I had heard Atari was coming out with an Asteroids cassette, so it seemed like a neat idea to have my own game. That way, I could avoid the street kids and have something interesting to do on weekends instead of watching TV. I had long since given up my rocket models.

I bought an Atari and two cassettes. Asteroids wasn't out yet, so I got Space Invaders and Combat. I figured out a way to make the thing fire double so I could get these real high scores. No one would play with me because I always won. Even when my friends came over, they would only play if I was on the same side with them. What was funny was how many adults liked to play the games. One of the soloists from Ballet Theatre came over and got so involved that he bought his own set a week later.

The strange thing about buying my own video game was that it didn't stop me from going out and playing the quarter machines. There were always machines with games I couldn't get on a cassette. And it was interesting to learn the rules of playing the public machines. You put down a stack of quarters and that told how many games you were going to play. If someone else wanted to play, he or she would put a stack of quarters behind yours, and when your stack was finished you were expected to give up the game or use your karate.

I often wished I really did know karate, not necessarily to use on anyone but just to know. I seemed to have had to fight for things in more ways than one that year. My work with the opera was going well, but my dancing was not improving as it should have been. After the injury the previous year, my jumps never seemed high enough and my turns weren't getting better. I actually felt I was getting worse.

I'm not sure just what was happening—whether I was growing or too busy with other things or what. I was still having problems with my arches, and my feet were not as strong as they should have been. As evaluation time neared at SAB, I was afraid I would be held back still another year. I just could not face studying with nine-year-olds again, especially now that I was almost fourteen.

With the help of a financial-aid program, I was able to get the money I needed to attend Professional Children's School the following fall. I had been accepted at Performing Arts High School, but the prospective tour with the opera was going to interfere with my schedule, so I had to turn them down. My major reason for attending PCS was that I hoped to be in the men's intermediate class at School of American Ballet. (The thought of being in A2 again was too depressing.) I didn't know what to do and was not ready to stop dancing.

It was definitely the turning point for me. Mom had a long talk with Jean-Pierre. He seemed to feel I was not going to make it as a dancer, at least not the way I was progressing at the time. He knew how much dancing meant to me and suggested that I give it at least another year somewhere else before I made a decision. But Mom decided to get several opinions and told me that if they were all negative, I should quit right away rather than frustrate myself for another year. Inside, I knew she was only thinking of my own good, but I was angry at her and very scared for myself. Mom set me up for an evaluation with Patricia Wilde at American Ballet Theatre School and Meredith Baylis at the Joffrey School. I was going to audition at Joffrey for a scholarship because Jean-Pierre had highly recommended another Frenchman named Jacques Cesbron as a teacher for me. Jacques taught the men's class at Joffrey.

The evaluations and biggest tests of my life were to come shortly after my graduation from Cathedral School. Compared to dance, schoolwork had been the easy part of my life, even that impossible Latin class. If only all the "A" grades could have been for my dancing, I would have been extremely happy.

At the awards banquet just before graduation, I received an honors certificate for my work in mathematics. I also got an award for French, which was probably the only subject that was remotely related to dance. I was proud of the French award because of all the trouble I had with the language at first. I had even considered going to France to study ballet sometime in the future, but Jean Pierre said I couldn't study at the Paris Opera unless I was a French citizen.

The graduation ceremony was the next day in the main cathedral. Thinking I would wear a long gown, I wore jeans. It was the dumbest thing I ever did at that school. It's a wonder they let me graduate that day. We had gowns, but they were short, and I really felt like a jerk as the twenty graduates waited to march to the cathedral altar for our diplomas. I looked around the inside of the cathedral and noticed how the sun was shining through the rose window. It is a beautiful big round window at the front of the cathedral. It is about twenty-five or more feet across and all stained glass. It's supposed to be one of the most beautiful rose windows in the world. Standing there looking at

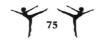

Graduation from Cathedral School was a sad day.

the window made me a little sad about leaving
school. In a way, I guess the graduation was not just
from a school but to a new way of life. I had already
graduated once in San Diego and moved to the east-
ern life-style. My sister always had to move the year
before her graduations and complained that I was
always graduating. She was probably right. Next fall I
would be in an artist's community of dancers, actors,
musicians, and other professionals. I just hoped I
would still be a dancer.

My name was called and I went up to get my diplo-
ma. At that point the only thing I was nervous about
was that everyone there was probably looking at my
jeans.

Horizons

By the time I graduated from Cathedral School, I was even further away from the New York City Ballet than before. I auditioned for the summer program at Saratoga, New York, which is connected with the City Ballet summer season. Two of my close friends and I wanted to go together to the upstate resort area, but only one of us was accepted. I was turned down. This was the first time I had failed an important audition, and my self-confidence as a dancer was beginning to fade as fast as my luck.

The next trial in store for me was to be the evaluation with Patricia Wilde at American Ballet Theatre. But before that took place, I had a class with Ivan Nagy, who taught at the school. It brought back memories of my visit to the Dorothy Chandler Pavilion when I was eight years old. That was when I was standing on a theater seat yelling "bravo" while he took bows after dancing in *La Sylphide*. Now here I was, taking a class from him.

Ivan is a tall man with green eyes, sandy-colored hair, and a Hungarian accent. He has a great sense of humor, especially when he demonstrated what some of us were doing wrong and moved crazily around the studio. His class was extremely difficult for me, and it was all I could do to keep up. Some of the combinations of steps were too advanced for my abilities, but I managed to finish the class. Ivan seemed to think I was doing fine and had some potential, but I could tell he didn't consider me particularly talented. I was hoping Miss Wilde would be more positive or Mom might really decide to talk me into quitting dance.

A few days later I took the scholarship class with Miss Wilde. I was more fortunate than I had been with Ivan because even though her classes were just as difficult, the combinations were very similar to the ones Jean-Pierre had given me all year and I was able to follow better.

I was worried all through the class, thinking that if Miss Wilde didn't like me I was really in trouble. She was very nice, but I couldn't tell how she felt about what I was doing. The other kids in the class were so much better than I was. I would have killed to have feet like a few of them. I kept wishing I had inherited my mom's high arches instead of Dad's flat feet.

When the class was over, Miss Wilde had a long talk with Mom and me. Generally, she was positive about my abilities and even said my feet were not as bad as I thought they were. She thought my main problem was in my placement or center of balance. I was lifting my hip to get my leg to raise higher and it was throwing off everything. My turns were awful—when I could get around at all. Miss Wilde said this was a common problem with growing teens and was easily corrected. I finally breathed a little easier. If I made it through the Joffrey audition, I had at least a year to prove myself.

Before that final trial, I had another opportunity to perform. This time it was with American Ballet Theatre. Because Mom worked for them, she always had inside information. This time she found out they were looking for a young boy around five foot one to work in their production of *Giselle*. She brought me in one Saturday, and the assistant stage manager said I would do fine. Rehearsals were to begin the following Monday. It would be a nondance role, but it would give me a chance to meet members of the company and observe how they operated as a performing group. I was supposed to be the barrel boy, a part that involved being dressed as the god of wine and carried out on a barrel by several guys in the corps. The corps

I was hoping to do well at the evaluation at American Ballet Theatre so Mom wouldn't try to talk me out of wanting to dance.

girls, dressed as village peasants, danced around me while I smiled and waved around a big wine cup and a bunch of fake grapes.

On Monday night, I had a huge surprise. Mr. Baryshnikov himself came out to show me my role! He walked up to me and asked if I was the barrel boy. I nodded. He demonstrated how I was to act on top of the barrel. The company performed the ballet that night with Baryshnikov in the lead role. Within the next two weeks I got to meet all the superstars like Cynthia Grégory, Natalia Makarova, Fernando Bujónes, and Alexander Gódunov.

One night was really funny. I had made friends with several guys in the corps and they pointed out the guys they didn't like. When I came out on the barrel, I threw plastic grapes down on them. I hit one guy on the head and my friends laughed. They said I was the best barrel boy they had that year.

After *Giselle* was over, Mr. Baryshnikov added a role for me in *Don Quixote*. I played a devilish little gypsy boy. During the first act, I went around the set getting in everyone's way, and in the second act I was part of a group in a gypsy camp. I didn't do much in that scene but sit around.

It was a lot of fun working with Ballet Theatre and I made some good friends. I also realized that if New York City Ballet didn't want me, there were possibilities with Ballet Theatre and Joffrey.

Soon after the performances with American Ballet Theatre I went to the Joffrey School for my audition. I was scheduled to take a two-hour intermediate class with Meredith Baylis and be considered for a winter scholarship. Without thinking about it, I dressed in the same T-shirt I had worn two years earlier for the audition at the School of American Ballet. It was the

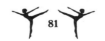

Nutcracker shirt I got when I danced with the San Diego Ballet. It was very short but it fit when I pulled up my tights with suspenders. I must have figured the shirt was lucky or something.

The barre section of class lasted an hour. I worked so hard to do everything correctly that I was practically exhausted by the time we got to center floor. Perspiration ran down my face like rain, not just from dancing but from being nervous. This was it. I knew I had to do well or it was the end of ballet for me. I wasn't doing very well either. The students in this class must have come all the time because Miss Baylis explained very little about the combinations, and everyone seemed to know exactly what she wanted—everyone but me. I kept up mostly by watching the students in front of me—something I always hate doing because if the person I copy is all messed up, I will be also.

With each new step in center floor my balance seemed to get worse and I was wobbling all over the place. Whatever else I had done wrong in my ballet career, this had to be the worst I had ever performed in a ballet class. I felt like I was doomed.

The last thing we did was big jumps, and I tried to keep up with the older boys. If anything was going to save me, it was this. I looked in the studio mirror and saw that I was doing all right. To the others, I must have finally looked as if I knew something about dance. I wasn't quite as freaked out over possibly being rejected, and I felt that I might at least have a small chance of still getting a scholarship.

When class was over, I went to the dressing room to change while Mom spoke with Edith D'Addario, the director of the school. I was afraid to go back out and find out the results. When I finally did, Mom told me

If I didn't get through the Joffrey audition, it was the end of my ballet career.

that even though I had done poorly, they had seen a lot of potential in me and were willing to give me a try. I walked out of the studio and down the stairs into the sunshine of Greenwich Village, feeling as though my life had been saved. I didn't even feel scared to go home alone. After asking Mom for a dollar, I left her and went to play a few games at the arcade. I felt I couldn't lose at anything.

I spent the rest of the summer in Minnesota with my dad. We went camping and fishing on the lake and I learned how to water ski and wind surf. I've always loved outdoor sports and I'm pretty good at them. But I have very fair skin and it's very difficult for me to get a suntan. Usually I burn, and sometimes it's so bad that my eyes become swollen shut. I always feel like a jerk when I have to go swimming in a T-shirt and long pants by the middle of the day. It's almost not worth going out, but I love the challenge of wind and water. My dad has always had some kind of sailboat, and I used to crew for him on weekends. There is nothing more exciting than to have the boat heeling way over in the water and be standing on the other side holding on. I wasn't as good at fishing. Usually, I would just sit there and watch everyone else reel the fish in. But even that was fun to me.

My sister and I returned to New York after the summer to discover that Mom was moving us all to New Jersey. We learned the news in the taxi on the way back from the airport. Neither of us knew quite what to say. But the more I thought about it, the more logical it seemed to be. The lease was up on our apartment and the rent was being raised to two hundred dollars more a month. Rents were getting so terrible that people couldn't afford to live in the city anymore unless they were rich (and we weren't).

The main problem was having to commute into the city from New Jersey. Mom had sent the car back to California with a friend soon after we arrived in New York. We would have to depend on public transportation. That meant we would be riding subway trains. The move took place a week later. Union City, New Jersey, was not exactly my idea of suburban living. Two years earlier, when we stayed in the motel before moving into our apartment, we were way out in the country. This new area was a Cuban settlement, at the other end of the Lincoln Tunnel, where hardly anyone spoke English. I never learned Spanish, and talking to anyone was extremely difficult. Living in Union City changed my life-style quite a lot, however, and mostly, it turned out, for the good.

Soon after we moved into the apartment—a ground-floor, two-bedroom place with lots of room—the boy upstairs came down to ask if I wanted to play softball. He was my age and, even though he was Cuban, he spoke excellent English. It was nice for me to be able to go outside and hang around a neighborhood without being afraid I would get mugged. My new friend and I played games at the video arcades and rode around on our bikes. I had enough money left over from my opera performances to afford an inexpensive bike. Most of my earnings had been spent on valuable stamps. My grandfather is a stamp collector and he got me started one Christmas when I was twelve. I have already put together an album of stamps that is worth over $4,000. Someday I hope to be able to afford a block of airplane stamps that is worth that much alone. Stamp collecting is a great thing because when people don't know what to give you for a present, you can always have them buy you a stamp.

Living in Union City wasn't too bad. In addition to

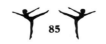

seeing my friend upstairs, I began to spend weekends with another friend from Professional Children's School. He had been in my class at SAB but quit to become an actor. At the time, he had the starring role in a small play. When I went to see him perform, I began to think more seriously about acting myself.

The opportunity came when my mom spoke with a lady from a management agency. The agency was looking for boys nine through fourteen to act in commercials and films. Since Ballet Theatre had no boys that young, she gave the lady a copy of the magazine article on me that had been written the year before. The next thing I knew, I was sitting in an office being interviewed.

They were definitely interested in me but felt I needed two things. The first and most important was a good photo, and the second was some acting lessons for what was called "cold readings" (being able to read a part from a script without studying it first). The photo would have to wait until my top braces came off. That was due to happen the first part of the following year. Mom found an acting coach to work with me for four months while we waited. Also, I began rehearsals once again for *The Cunning Little Vixen*.

As if I didn't already have enough to do, I met a friend of my mom's who was a banjo player. Since his apartment was right near the Joffrey School, I used to go there when I had extra time between classes. The first time I went was when there was a power blackout in half of the city. None of the trains were running, so thousands of people left work early to try and catch a bus. We didn't have any lights in the studio at Joffrey, so we were also excused early that day. I walked out to the street, which was a mob of people

One of my best friends at Joffrey was Jeremy.

and slow-moving cars, and watched buses go by that were so tightly packed with people they were almost bursting. I decided there was no way I was going to get home, so I went to Jack's house where he was giving a banjo lesson to someone.

I had never played an instrument before and I became interested in trying. Mom had bought me a flute for my eleventh birthday but we had never found a teacher or the time for lessons. When Jack offered to teach me the banjo, I decided that was for me. My mom's dad had been a terrific banjo player and I guess I kind of hoped it was hereditary. I picked the basics up quickly. The only problem was that I didn't have a lot of time to learn or practice, so I never progressed much. Maybe someday in the future I will try again.

It seemed at this time that my whole life changed for the better. I loved my classes at Joffrey, and for the first time since we moved to the East Coast, I had lots of good friends. My classmates at Professional Children's School were mostly other dancers and we had a lot in common. One of my friends was a girl named Melissa Colgate. She was a student at American Ballet Theatre School. We had fun comparing notes on our different classes, especially since she had also gone to School of American Ballet. Some of my non-dancing friends were in soap operas, television situation comedies, commercials, movies, and Broadway plays. When I found out how much money the actors made, I became even more interested in theater. By that time, my acting coach had given me lots of different kinds of scripts. She was an extremely nice lady who also worked in soap operas.

I remember one night that was really funny. Mom came storming into my room ready to get after Stephanie and me for arguing. My sister and I *were* yelling at each other, but it was because I was rehearsing one of my scripts. I think Mom felt foolish when she discovered what we were doing. I guess sometimes I looked pretty silly myself, like when I would walk into the kitchen saying something like, "Does your cat like to go off and think sometimes?" Everyone would have a blank expression for a moment as if thinking I had finally flipped out. Then they would realize I was just practicing again.

There was another incident I remember that wasn't so funny. I was on my way to my acting lesson in a very nice neighborhood when I noticed a group of young guys on a street corner. Unfortunately, they noticed me too, and I started to run. They came after me and caught me in the middle of the block. They pushed me into the entrance hall of a brownstone. The biggest of them held onto me while three others went through all my pockets. There was this one little jerk who was about ten or twelve years old. He kept swearing and punching me. He hit me in the eye and then took my new wallet, my subway pass, and the check I had for my acting teacher. One of the others wanted my book bag, but somehow I managed to convince him that it was just full of schoolbooks. Then they tried to take my jacket. That was when I broke away from them and ran all the way to my teacher's apartment. While I was running, I looked back once and noticed the group had grabbed another kid. I was so furious I couldn't see straight. I kept thinking about that little punk hitting me and taking my wallet and how helpless I had been with those others holding me against the wall. I wanted to somehow get back at them.

My acting teacher called the police and I spent an hour giving a report while they filled out papers. Then I took a cab to the Joffrey School for my afternoon dance class. When I got there and began to talk to some of the other boys in the class, I realized they all had mugging stories of their own. Somehow I felt better knowing I wasn't alone. Even some of the bigger guys had stories to tell. Size doesn't matter when six punks jump you. Fortunately, it isn't something that happens all the time. One thing I realized was that this time I was not so scared. I guess the city was making me tough.

I was making some good friends at Joffrey. Since I was no longer in a group of little boys, the classes were more of a challenge to me. Jacques was a good teacher, and I was thankful to Jean-Pierre for recommending him. I was making progress with my dancing, and my balance was much better. After Jacques's class I would take a class with Meredith Baylis. There were girls in that class and it was much different from my other ones. Whenever I came out of her classes, I felt like everything had been stretched.

The studio at Joffrey is not a big modern fancy place like those at the other major schools, but the training was no less professional. I was really happy at Joffrey. They gave us free tickets for the company performances and I loved the things they did. A lot of their ballets are more modern, and everyone seems to be having a great time dancing. Mom and I used to compare the three major ballet companies to paintings. The New York City Ballet was like a piece of modern art with lines and colors. The American Ballet Threatre was classical like an old master's painting of trees and meadows. And the Joffrey was somewhere in between like those paintings with lots of little dots. When I wasn't dancing or playing video games, I would go to art museums. That was one of the real advantages of living in New York City. It has so many great things to see and do.

The opera had begun its winter season and I was back into rehearsals for *The Cunning Little Vixen*. It was strange getting into that hawk costume again. Lots of my friends from the year before were too big for their costumes. A few of them became larger animals and some of them quit. Doing the hawk role was

At Joffrey I was no longer in a group of little boys. Here I am with Brian and Marcus.

easy for me. Since I wasn't learning where to go or what to do anymore, I was able to concentrate on moving more like a bird.

We played six performances in New York City and then went to California once again. This time it was not as much fun because the boys were so much younger. Also there were a lot more kids and we were more carefully watched. We went to Disneyland again and then to the La Brea Tar Pits and museum. The tar pits were not very interesting. I guess I expected to see struggling dinosaur skeletons coming out of them or something. They were just pools of mucky stuff that I guess was tar. The skeletons were inside the museum. I had already seen many of the dinosaurs at the American Museum of Natural History in New York. Being at the museum in Los Angeles made me realize that some things in the two cities were not so far apart.

Since most of the other boys were so young, I spent much of my spare time with video games. By this time, my favorite game was Donkey Kong. The first time I had played it I didn't understand how to get through the obstacle course. Neither could my friend, Matthew. We got through the first level because that involved only jumping over barrels, but the second level had more to it. Finally, by accident, Matt made the tower collapse and we had the solution. I don't know how many quarters I spent trying to get through more than two levels. Those games are really addictive.

Performing at the Dorothy Chandler was not as exciting as it had been the year before. There was a great deal of sadness for me. I called Nana to say hello, but she wasn't able to come see me perform because she was very ill. Less than four weeks later, she died. It was the first time I had lost someone close to me and I had all kinds of mixed feelings. I was at least happy she had seen me dance the year before and had accepted me as an artist. That meant a lot to me. It's nice to know after someone is gone that she appreciated you and that you had shown you had accomplished something important to carry on in the family.

The week before Christmas, Mom tried to keep the holidays as bright as possible by having another tree-trimming party for the American Ballet Theatre students. Mom and Stephanie and I had gone to a tree lot near our apartment and found a large fir. Snow was everywhere, and walking back with the tree made me feel like it was really winter. I had always hated Christmas in California, when the radio would be playing songs about snowmen and sleigh rides and Jack Frost nipping your nose and the temperature would be ninety degrees. People would actually be barbequing turkeys on grills in the backyard! Buying a Christmas tree in California usually involved driving to the local nursery and bringing the tree home in the trunk of the car. I loved being in the East where we could carry the tree over our shoulders and come into the house smelling like pine needles.

The party was fun. I had a chance to get better acquainted with Melissa Colgate. She told me about her crazy schedule at American Ballet Theatre while we spent most of the afternoon playing a new Atari cassette called Skiing. We talked a lot about dance and even agreed to dance together in a small performance in the next year. Both of us were anxious about the coming year. Melissa had heard rumors that Ballet

Nineteen eighty-two was going to be a year of changes for me.

Theatre was signing on dancers from other places, and I was not certain whether or not Mom would stay in the East after the lease was up on the New Jersey apartment. That would mean I had to find a way to stay in New York on my own or maybe give up my career. However things went, Melissa and I knew for certain that 1982 was going to be a year of big changes for both of us.

New Horizons

For the Christmas holidays of 1981 Stephanie and I stayed with Dad. We flew to Utah and went skiing at Park City, which is one of the better places for that winter sport. I love skiing because it always came easy to me. It is also one of the worst things a dancer can do. Not only do I use all the wrong muscles, but the danger of twisting a knee or breaking a leg is great. Lots of ballet schools make you sign a contract stating that you will not participate in any outside activity that will interfere with dance training and be a hazard. Skiing is the first activity on that list. But since I hadn't signed anything like that with the Joffrey School, I decided I could still go and I prayed I wouldn't get hurt.

I was around ten years old the first time I went skiing. My dad put me in a beginner's class on the bunny hill and went off to ski on his own. When he came back for me, I was gone. He found me riding up the big chair lift with one of the instructors about to take my second run down the big hill. I pointed the skis straight down and somehow still had control. Snow flew everywhere. I loved the feeling of going so fast without being in some kind of vehicle. I've never been hurt and don't plan on giving up the sport either. It's too much fun.

In early January, Patricia Wilde said I could come back to American Ballet Theatre for another evaluation and consideration as a possible candidate for their summer program. At the time I thought Joffrey was like SAB in that they discouraged the winter students in the summer, so I was looking around for someplace to go in the six-week summer session.

I took the morning class with twelve scholarship students, and right away knew I was in for a challenge because I was standing behind another guest who happened to be a former principal dancer from American Ballet Theatre. The first thing I realized was that I was not very limber. Everyone in the class could do the splits every which way and had feet that pointed and arched like boomerangs. Unlike the class I had taken the year before with Miss Wilde, the combinations this time did not come easily to me and I constantly made mistakes. Also, my friend Melissa was in the class and I felt very self-conscious about doing so badly.

When the class was over, I was not at all surprised by what Miss Wilde told me. After complimenting me on my improved balance, she went on to say that my feet had become worse and I was not using them properly. She would not commit herself about the summer program, but told me to return for an audition in the spring. This meant I would come back with the "cattle call" audition.

I was not too encouraged by her evaluation, yet I seemed to do well and was liked at Joffrey. One thing I began to realize was that one person's opinion was not necessarily the only opinion. I did take Miss Wilde's advice, however, and began working harder on my feet, using all the muscles and going "through" the feet. This means stepping through one set of muscles at a time rather than just bending the foot in one movement. Doing that strengthens the foot and makes the combination look smoother.

I tried two more summer auditions. The first was for the program in Saratoga. I had tried out the year before. About one hundred girls and thirty boys showed up and they accepted lots of the girls and about six boys. I was not one of the boys, even though

I always felt self-conscious about dancing badly.

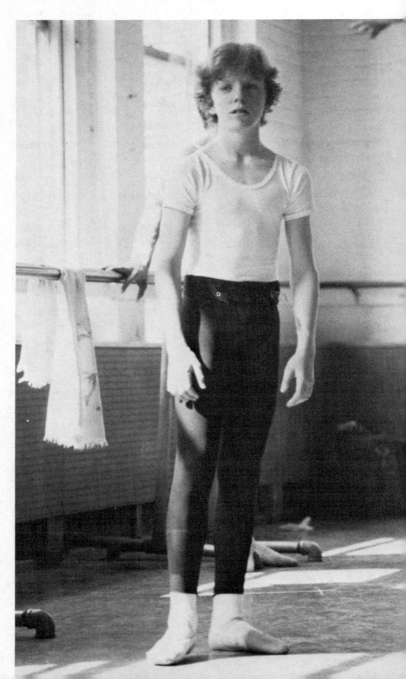

I lasted until the final elimination. At that point, I guess I knew I would never be City Ballet material.

The other audition was for the San Francisco Ballet school. Going there seemed like a fun idea. I would live in a dormitory and be on my own, kind of like the time I was in Los Angeles with the opera.

I did a lot better at this audition. About a hundred and fifty students showed up, and they accepted around thirty. Because there were so many of us, we went in two groups. I was still young enough to be in the fourteen and under class, which was probably an advantage. I always look worse when I am competing with older students, especially girls. Girls are more limber and can usually raise their legs up to their ears.

The director of the San Francisco Ballet school gave us a one-hour class. I made my mother swear not to say anything to him about me being her son. Mom knew him, and I didn't want to think he accepted me because of her. As it turned out, he found out anyway, but not until after I was accepted. They offered me a half-scholarship and I would have taken it, but I hadn't planned on the expense of getting to San Francisco. Even with my airline pass, the cost was too much, because I also had to pay for room and board. I didn't have enough of my own money and Mom couldn't afford it either.

At the time I didn't have any performances with the opera. I was hoping now to make money with commercials. In February I got my top braces off and my teeth looked terrific. Everyone said I looked like a different kid without all the hardware. Mom made an appointment to get my pictures taken.

My self-image improved after I got rid of the braces on my teeth.

The photo session was a lot of fun. I had never worked with a professional photographer before and didn't know what to do. Before I went in to have pictures taken, I met with the photographer. He showed me an album of the work he had already done, so I could see how skilled he was and also so I would know what he expected of me. I was instructed to show up the next time with a suitcase full of clothes, including a hat, so he could try all kinds of different ideas for a special look for me. The photo would only be from the shoulders up, but from what I saw of the other pictures he had taken, the outfit made all the difference in the way the personality showed through.

The photographer also used all kinds of lighting and even a fan to blow my hair around. Sometimes I would look like a real punk and in other pictures I was very serious. I even had on my reading glasses in one of them.

We got the photos back a week later and they were very good. There were several that were by far the best pictures ever taken of me, and no one could decide which ones to use. Finally, we had two of them made up with my name on the bottom just like the kind some people get when they ask for a fan picture of a movie star. We gave most of them to my manager to use to set up auditions for me.

When I wasn't in school or ballet classes, I was out with my friend from upstairs shoveling snow for five dollars a walkway. I also used to drop by and see my friend Jack. I wasn't doing much with the banjo lessons, but we would go to one of his friends' apartments and have Monopoly tournaments. Most of his friends worked in television and were very interesting. They also played a mean game of Monopoly.

By April, I was cast in another opera. It was a new production called *La Grand Duchesse de Gérolstein*. It was probably one of my most exciting dance roles. I played a soldier, and six of us did an entire three-minute dance. The opera was a comedy and had some very funny props like this huge cloud that would lower down from way up in the theater. It had two

giant hands holding it and a sword that the hero would take whenever he went off to battle. According to the schedule, *Grand Duchesse* was also going to California the following fall.

When I wasn't performing, I spent the weekends with my actor friend Matthew. Both his parents were in theater and we once went to see his dad in a play. We also went to the movies a lot. We must have seen every film that was released that year, some of them twice. Both of us went to the video arcade a lot too. During the week, I would stop at the arcade on my way home from ballet class and then call Matt to see what high score he had gotten on his way home. We were still into Donkey Kong. But now we were getting the highest scores. I was so into arcade games that when I didn't have a quarter to play, I would sometimes watch the demonstration.

Mom was starting to talk about moving back to California. I wanted to stay in New York, and she said if I could find a living arrangement that she felt was good, I might be able to remain. I was going to be fifteen in June, but she felt I was too young to live on my own with her so far away. The only person she approved of me staying with was Jack. He was all for the idea, but his apartment was too small and he would have to find another one. He was going to have to find another apartment anyway, because they were selling his building, but he wasn't sure he could get anything quickly enough for me to move into by fall. So everything was up in the air. I knew I couldn't go back to California without setting back my dance career at least a year. I didn't know what to do. I just kept hoping Jack would find something.

Jeremy and I spent lots of time in the video arcades.

After the opera, I had another opportunity to perform. Mom heard that the Royal Danish Ballet was coming to New York to perform at the Met and they needed extras. I went to the theater and met some of the Royal Danish people. I was too tall for what they needed, but not too many boys showed up, probably because it was during school hours. They chose me for a ballet called *Napoli Act III* and fitted me into a peasant costume with a huge hat, a vest, a full-sleeved shirt, and knee pants. I looked like someone out of the fifteenth century. All I needed was a long pole and a gondola to complete the picture. This was supposed to be a ballet set in Naples, Italy, so we had to stand on a bridge constructed over the back section of the stage and wave our hats after each dance. The next night we were to have our first performance. As extras, we were paid $5 for each performance and $5 for each rehearsal. The actual dancing was done by company members and children they had brought with them from Denmark.

I liked the Royal Danish Ballet. They have a style that is called Bournónville, where they hold their bodies in a certain controlled way and wear beautiful bright costumes. The ballet I was in had one tarantella after the other. A tarantella is a fast, wild folk dance that takes a lot of coordination and strength. It is very exciting to watch.

The Royal Danish children seemed snobbish at first, but I soon realized it was because they were from a foreign country and we were strangers to them. A lot of them spoke very good English and they asked us all kinds of questions about the ballet schools in America. I was very interested in their school and wished I could go there, but you have to be a Danish citizen to attend the royal school. I don't even have any Danish ancestors, even though I am blond.

The set for our ballet was beautiful. Not only was there the bridge where we stood, but the entire stage looked like an outdoor garden. Most of the principals of the Royal Danish Ballet performed and the rest of us cheered. At the end of the scene, we had baskets of confetti that we threw down in handfuls. One of the little kids accidentally threw his hat and the girl next to me lost her basket. The dancers down below were very clever. As if it was part of the show, they tossed the hat and basket back up to us.

We had about six performances before the company left the city. I began to see just how lucky I was, being able not only to see these famous companies but also to work with them and meet them. I knew if I went back to California none of this would be as easily available to me.

I auditioned again for the American Ballet Theatre summer program and was one of about seventy fellows from twelve to twenty-five in age. We were judged by representatives from the school, the first and second companies. The class was only an hour, but I was there all day because I was in the call-backs and had to wait for the second group to audition. Then we had another hour class with the call-backs. I stayed right to the end of the audition before I was cut. I didn't know whether to be disappointed or not. Since I stayed so long I knew some of the people liked me. Later I found out they were the judges from the first company. Being cut put me right back where I started—wondering what school would take me for the summer.

The dumb part of all of this was that I should have asked the Joffrey School director right in the beginning if I could be in their summer program. I didn't think to ask because I thought they were going to have only one class a day. When I did ask, I realized I was expected to stay and that it was going to be one of the best programs of all, taught by some famous guest teachers and offering a number of classes. Besides ballet technique, I would also get character classes and pas de deux (two people dancing together). I had never been able to study pas de deux before because I was so small, but the summer program was going to have a lot of girls my height and shorter.

In the meantime, my mom was planning on remarrying, and our household was turned upside down with wedding plans. She arranged to be married in the Cathedral of St. John the Divine and I was the ring bearer. I liked the man she was marrying. Several of my school friends had stepparents who were awful to them. They used to come over to my house a lot just to get away from home.

I finished up my year at Professional Children's School and did very well. Mom got a notice that I was on the honor roll. They asked if I would be returning in the fall. I couldn't give them an answer then, so they gave me an extension on replying. Dad said he would pay for my schooling, but I had no place to stay. Jack still hadn't found a new apartment, and some of my friends' families said they would like to have me but didn't have any extra room. The only other alternative to my situation was to go to Salt Lake City and live with Dad. Ballet West has a school there that many people have said is pretty good. I was sure it was better than anything I could find in San Diego, where Mom was going to go. But I really didn't want to go to Salt Lake City either. I didn't know what I was going to do.

I only had a two-week break before I began summer school at Joffrey. Most of that time I spent wind surfing with my dad in Minnesota. Wind surfing was one of the most difficult and frustrating water sports I ever learned. I spent half my time climbing back on the board and the other half just trying to stay on my feet. The more wind there was, the more fun the wind surfing was, but it was also ten times more difficult. Even though I was in Minnesota for only two weeks, I got pretty good by the time I returned to New York. Whenever I came back to New York after being out in the county, it took a while for me to readjust. Everything is so much faster and crazier in the city. Even though I love New York, I don't know if I'll ever get used to the noise.

The summer school schedule was different from the one I had in the winter. I had to get up early and catch a bus about 7 A.M. into the city. The scholarship class began at 8:30, and if I caught all the buses and trains, I would get there with a half hour to get dressed and warm up. The scholarship class was two hours long. After that I would get a fifteen-minute break before I had another two-hour class. Then I would get a two-hour lunch break.

At first, I was at a loss for things to do during that long break. Sometimes I would go visit Jack, but he taught at the university three days a week. I started hanging around with a boy in the class named Jeremy. Sometimes we would go to Washington Square park and eat our lunches. That is the wildest and weirdest place in Greenwich Village. I don't think I have ever seen so many strange characters in one place in my life. There are people in costumes, people playing musical instruments, sometimes whole musical groups, people with green hair, bums sleeping on the lawn, lots of people playing chess on little stone tables, and creeps selling drugs. Jeremy and I would eat our lunches and watch everything like it was a circus. In addition to all the weirdos, there would also be ordinary people like ourselves, roller skaters, joggers, and mothers letting their little kids play in a special children's area. Some people would be sitting around in business suits getting a little sun before they had to go back to work, and other people would be walking their dogs.

The afternoon classes varied each day. Sometimes we had character and sometimes we had pas de deux. Jeremy and I used to get angry sometimes in pas de deux, because there would be these big macho guys who would partner all the little skinny girls and Jeremy and I would get stuck with girls twice our height and too heavy for us to lift. I did learn a lot about the timing of pas de deux. If the timing is off, it throws the girl off balance. Some of the girls we worked with were not very stong on pointe and we had to practically hold them up.

Character class was fun, but it was hard. I had never had character before, and I was a total klutz with the steps. The barre work in character is very different from ballet. There is a lot of heel-toe and kicking with the hands held on the hips and the head tilted to the side. The teacher was very patient with me and I enjoyed the class, but the first two weeks of the program I was exhausted. I would come home and lay down on the sofa and be sound asleep before dinner. Not only did we have the afternoon class, which was two hours, but an additional two-hour technique class after that. Some days we would end up dancing eight hours. We weren't required to take all the classes, but I wanted to get the most out of the program that I could.

I was usually tired on weekends too, but not too tired to go to the movies with Matt or have Jeremy over to throw around a frisbee. The one highlight of Union City was a huge monastery that was no longer

Some days we would end up dancing for eight hours.

in use. It had beautiful large grounds where we could go to picnic or play ball and frisbee. It was surrounded by big shade trees and even had a small cemetery. It was kind of interesting to read the headstones. A few of the monks who had lived there had been born in the 1800s.

We also had a kind of backyard outside our apartment, and we would have barbeques in the evening and watch the fireflies after it got dark. Since I was not working shows of any kind then, I had evenings free.

My acting career never got off the ground. Part of the reason was that I didn't have enough time, and the other was that my manager never got me any auditions. My friend Matt was doing really well. He got a TV commericial and a small part on a soap opera. I met with my manager and decided to break the contract so I could find an agent. But trying to find an agent when I didn't even know if I would stay in New York seemed pointless, so I just let things go. I did continue my acting lessons.

As the summer passed, I realized more and more that I wasn't going to be able to stay in New York. I wasn't sure what to do. Even though I liked staying with Mom, I felt I might ruin my dance career if I did stay with her. The only other choice was to stay with Dad. I finally made the decision that I had to dance, so I would go live with him.

After a year, I would be sixteen and would return to New York. By that time, Jack said, he would definitely have a place where maybe I could stay. I talked to Miss D'Addario at the Joffrey School and she said I could always come back. Miss Purintin at Professional Children's School said the same thing. But I was still miserable. I didn't want to leave. My whole life had never been as good as it had been this past year. All my friends were professionals or people who at least understood my dancing. The training at Joffrey was terrific. Jacques told me I had improved a lot since I first came there. New York was where I wanted to be

I may never have known my potential without Jacques.

and where I felt I belonged. But I was too young to stay alone and I understood my Mom was not taking me away to be mean.

In the middle of August I packed all my things and went to the airport with Mom and her new husband. They put me on a flight to Salt Lake City with advice to give my new life a chance to be good. I never felt so alone as when I got on that plane. It didn't seem like it was three years since I had come to New York. I truly hoped the time would go even faster until I returned.

As the New York City skyline passed by below me, I began to feel a little better. I knew New York would always be there for me as a friend, and maybe, someday, the stages at Lincoln Center would have the spotlight on me.

MELISSA

Every Little Girl Takes
Ballet Lessons

My first ballet lesson was not much of a success. I was close to tears the whole time. I was put into a difficult class and was unable to do what I thought were terribly complicated steps. Everyone seemed to know what they were doing but me. I didn't want my mother to know how upset I was so I acted like the lesson was just wonderful when she picked me up. Now practically my whole life is ballet.

There are four children in my family, but none of them are children anymore. I am the youngest and was born in Baton Rouge, Louisiana. Six months later, our family moved to New Jersey, where my father worked as an executive for a large company. Mom is a hard-working and wonderful mother who always felt children should have every advantage. She believed that all of us should be given the opportunity to study music and dance. Even my older brother took ballet for about six months. But I was the only one who took dance seriously. I had that scary first lesson at the age of four.

Lots of ballet teachers believe you shouldn't start that early because ballet is so serious and can be a real turn-off for a little kid. I don't think Mom wasted her time and money, because my teacher, Eve Lynn, was patient with me. Once I began to understand what I was doing, I enjoyed classical ballet a lot.

I also began tap-dancing classes, but I got out of those as soon as I could. Mom didn't have ambitions to make me a child star. She just wanted me to have musical ability and grace.

When I was six, my father was transferred to Los Angeles. The two years we spent there were a trial for all of us, but some of it turned out all right in the end. Actually, I don't remember too much about that time. I know mostly what Mom told me.

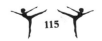

Good ballet lessons were scarce in our neighborhood, and the only place to take them was at what a lot of dancers call a Dolly Dinkle school. That is a corner school run by a dancer who never became famous. I was lost in this group of kids. Very few of them were serious. Ballet was something they took along with a dozen other things so they could get movie auditions. I just wanted to dance.

On the advice of a friend of my mom's, I was taken to one of the larger schools in Los Angeles. We went up a long stairway to a large old studio with high, beamed ceilings. Through the windows, I could smell bread baking. The two Russian women who ran the school were very interested in me. They said I had good possibilities and a nice dancer's body. I am lucky to have legs that look twice as long as the rest of my body.

With dancers, body type can be a very tricky thing. Sometimes nice proportions change when you start to grow, and a thin person can turn chubby with weird bulges everywhere. Lots of girls who have trained hard for years can be turned away at a critical time because of that.

The worst problem we had with the new school was the commute. Mom almost killed herself driving 120 miles a day. She not only took me to my ballet class but chauffeured my brother and sisters to other lessons. On top of that, she had only a half hour to get me from school to ballet class and we had to drive in rush-hour traffic. I always just barely made it in time. Finally, it was too much for everyone, and I had to return to the other ballet school.

During the ages of six and seven, I lost out on my ballet training, but I did other things. Since most of

116

my friends at school were members of the Brownies scout troop, I joined too. I can't say I remember much about it except trying to sell cookies. It was really terrifying to knock on doors and not know what kind of a person would answer. The people were usually nice, but sometimes there would be a crab who would almost make me cry. I was glad when I didn't have to sell anything anymore.

One thing I remember that I liked a lot during those years was the gymnastics training I had. We did somersaults, cartwheels, and backbends, and I was finally able to do splits. You could say that it was to my advantage not to have had ballet training then because I wouldn't have learned these other skills so easily. In addition to gymnastics, I also enrolled in an experimental theater program at UCLA during the summer. I studied the basics of performing and learned a lot about stagecraft. I also learned how to listen to music. UCLA has a huge campus and they have a terrific theater. For me it was like being somewhere really important like the Metropolitan Opera House in New York.

I should also probably mention the piano lessons. Everyone I know has had piano lessons sometime in her childhood and I was no exception. I studied for four years and hated it. I used to cry in the car on the way to my lessons because I didn't want to go. At home, when Mom thought I was downstairs practicing, I used to fool around and waste time. Mom thought I was doing well and I guess I did okay, but I sure didn't like it.

I have to admit now that even though I was not destined to be a great concert pianist, the lessons did improve my sense of music. A dancer who has no feel-

ing for rhythm or melody will never make it out of the corps of a large company—if he or she makes it into the corps at all.

When I was eight, Mom had finally had enough of Southern California and the million-mile commutes, and she talked Dad into getting a transfer back to New Jersey.

I went back to my first ballet school, but I also continued lessons in other things. One summer I went to a gymnastics camp. I also joined a theater group where I studied mime and voice and did musicals. I got the lead in productions of *Cinderella*, *Charlotte's Web*, and an original production titled *Broadway, Broadway* where I sang "What I Did for Love." But theater was not my thing, and I don't even remember much about what I did or how I felt about the productions. What I do remember was my first *Nutcracker*.

Dad said several years later that once the *Nutcracker* performances began, the family *never* had a Christmas. I was taken to rehearsals and performances all through the holidays and that included Christmas Eve. I was a clown in the second act and a child in the party scene of the first act. The party scene is mostly mime. We spend the entire time pretending we are having a wonderful time at a Christmas party. It's probably interesting from the audience, but it's really the pits unless you are Clara, the lead role. I wanted to play Clara so badly, I could have killed for the part a few years later, but the closest I ever came was to be an understudy once.

At the age of ten I began my first pointe (toe) class. Most little girls dream of the moment they go on toe, since that is the ideal of being a ballerina. Only when they are standing in those unbending shoes do they realize toe work is much more pain than pleasure.

The shoes themselves are a heavy cloth coated with Fiberglass. The shank (or hard part of the sole) is stiff leather and the body of the shoe is pink satin. With the ribbons sewn on, the shoe is a beautiful work of art and it makes the foot look terrific. A wise teacher will not put a student on toe until the foot and ankle are strong enough. Going on toe too soon can not only destroy the growth and structure of the feet, it can throw off the whole body. Sometimes overeager mothers try to force a ballet teacher to put their daughters on toe. They seem to think if another girl their daughter's age is on toe, their daughter is ready too. It's really a mean thing to do to a kid.

It's funny now to look at old pictures of me on toe. I have to laugh. I looked so weak and ridiculous. Oddly, I was never too interested in watching ballet on television or going to New York to see live performances at Lincoln Center. Like most of my dance friends, I idolized Mikhail Baryshnikov and had his picture in my room. At the time, he and Rudolph Nureyev were the two most well-known male dancers in this country.

This story of my dance training sounds like I wasn't much of a normal kid, but I did do all kinds of crazy things with my friends from school. I was a really good tree climber, probably because of my long legs. We had great trees on our property, and I loved to see how close to the top I could get. It's a wonder I didn't break my neck. Once when my parents were away, I tried to drive their truck but I didn't get very far. Something went wrong with the engine, and it scared me so much that I didn't try it again. Luckily I hadn't gone far enough for them to notice. I got in trouble for other little mischievious things, but generally I was pretty much an ordinary kid when I wasn't slaving away in the ballet studio.

My teachers constantly encouraged me in dance class. When I was twelve, I took eleven classes a week. My body had not changed its shape, and there was every reason to believe it would stay that of a classical ballerina. My legs were the same length as those of some girls four inches taller than I was. For anything other than dance (or climbing trees), I probably looked out of proportion.

Every year, kids from all over the United States come to New York thinking they will be immediately accepted into a large school or company. Most of them are the best in their classes in some unknown school, and they think they have little more to learn. It is sad, because when they arrive in New York, rejection comes like a swift kick with the hard end of a pointe shoe. No one wants them or cares. The major reason for elimination is body type. If a girl is overweight or looks wrong, she is not considered, no matter how talented she is. Plus, many girls are trained wrong and have bad habits.

Thousands of girls want to be ballerinas, compared with the hundreds of boys who want to be what is called a danseur. Boys have a better chance, but even they are facing stronger competition now. They are eliminated for the same reasons as girls.

Everyone who had seen me dance so far had agreed I has some talent, but this wasn't enough for Mom. She gave me an ultimatum: either I was accepted by the School of American Ballet or no more classes. My studying dance had already involved a great deal of time and money. Even though my parents were well off financially, they still had three other children to think about. My second to oldest sister was in law school and about to graduate first in her class, and my older brother was going to a special ski camp to train for the Olympics.

Now that I had a toe class daily, I was in constant need of shoes. Pointe shoes run $32 a pair and are worn out in a week. During a performance, some dancers go through several pairs, depending on their roles. At $32 a pair, a dancer could go broke in a short time without financial help.

I got the idea that the secret to being an instant ballet superstar was to be a Russian defector. I never would have had any problems if I had studied in Russia. I thought if I could go to Russia and study there a few years until I was good, I could defect to the United States and everyone would want to hire me. That's how silly I was.

By the time I went to audition for the School of American Ballet, I was so involved in my dancing that I could not have even dreamed of quitting. Like many other girls my age, I had seen the movie *The Turning Point* with Leslie Browne and Mikhail Baryshnikov. I not only wanted to live that dream but I wanted to meet them and work with them.

My first step was to go to New York City to take the School of American Ballet (SAB) audition. I was seen with twenty other students in an abbreviated class that included standard barre technique (exercises done while holding the ballet barre). These included pliés (like deep knee bends), tendues (stretching of the feet), and rond de jambes (circular movements with legs and feet). The center floor part of the audition included adagio (slow controlled movements), pirouettes (turns), and small and large jumps.

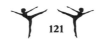

The girls were selected on body type, limberness, strength, and their general "look." A girl could have a few flaws, but if she was an interesting dance personality, she would be considered.

I didn't have an interesting dance personality, and I was scared to death. Luckily, I did have a good body and was limber from the gymnastics. But the pressure was on. To not be accepted would mean the end of my career and, to me, the meaning of my life.

Two Russian women discussed the auditioning students in Russian, so no one knew how he or she was being judged. I got the idea I was doing okay because I hadn't messed up on anything we had to perform. I noticed some of the other students had trouble with combinations, so I had a little confidence—but not much. I wondered what the women were saying about me.

After the audition was over, we waited outside the office as each mother was called in by the director. I sat on a long plastic sofa and perspired while I waited what seemed like an hour but was really only five minutes. I kept thinking, what if she says no, what then? What would I do? There was nothing else I wanted to do. Nothing. Then Mom returned, smiling and holding a summer schedule. I was laughing and crying at the same time. My ballet career was gong to continue.

The summer session at the School of American Ballet began a whole new life for me. It was an introduction to the pattern my dance career would follow for the next two years. I studied with most of the instructors at the school. All of them were Russian or former members of the New York City Ballet. There were forty other girls in my class. Most of the time I felt lost in the crowd or shoved behind a pillar while a fringe

Luckily I had a good body and was limber from all the gymnastics classes I took when I was younger.

of mothers sat and watched their daughters push their way to the front.

I don't want to sound conceited, because I'm not certain myself why other students and their mothers were always mean to me. I guess whatever I did well showed too much, and they wanted to discourage me. Mothers seemed to see me as a professional threat to their daughters. Really, I felt like anything but a threat. I still had too much to learn.

The reason I bring this up is that I remember one time in particular when I took a pointe class. The mothers were all on the sidelines, watching us as usual, and I was not having a good class. Nothing went well for me and I was almost in tears. We did this one especially difficult combination and I fell. One of the mothers actually stood up and applauded! Then she took her finger and drew it down as though she was keeping an invisible score on me. I was so embarrassed and upset that I ran crying out of the studio.

The director and one of the other teachers had me in the office consoling me and telling me they would do something about what had happened. They did too. Not only did they ban the mothers from the studios, but they made them wait down the hall. Obviously not all ballet mothers were like that. It was too bad the nice ones had to be excluded. Later, mothers were allowed to watch class, but only by appointment.

The summer program at SAB included two classes a day plus a character class. In character we learned the basic steps of folk dancing, which are almost always in full-length ballets. I was in level one, which is the lowest class of that section. Five was the highest.

The biggest problem I had was concentration, because sometimes I didn't find the class challenging enough. When they asked me to stay for the winter session, they wanted me in children's level five, which is one class lower. Mom said I was too young to stay in the city anyway, so that was the end of that. I was going to have to wait until I was fourteen, another year, before I came to New York. I knew that was the only place to be to become a professional dancer.

I went back to studying in New Jersey. I had to bide my time. We had commuted all summer, but Mom was not about to do that again, especially when the weather turned bad. I also went back to one of my most frustrating performing experiences.

Soon afterward the *Nutcracker* was cast for the holiday season. It was my third, and I was sick of being a clown in the second act and a child in that very boring party scene. I wanted to be Clara so bad I couldn't see straight. The whole ballet is about her, even though she doesn't do a whole lot of dancing except in the beginning. I think every little girl dreams of doing that part at least once.

They chose someone from another company to dance the part of Clara, and four understudies were selected from the students. I lived an hour and a half away from the studio and had to be there for every rehearsal. But I never once got to dance the part with the company people. After all that, only one of the four understudies got to perform and it wasn't me.

I had learned the part well. We performed mostly in high school auditoriums and gymnasiums. Even one performance anywhere would have been fine with me, just to get to do it once and say I had officially been Clara. But it wasn't meant to be, I guess. I have to admit I was terribly disappointed, but through all the frustration, my mom gave me one piece of good advice. She said that I was never to show anger to my teachers no matter how I felt.

As long as I can remember, I cannot recall ever having real stage fright. I guess its because I love to perform. Once onstage, I just forget there's an audience. Also, I don't think it is the same as an audition, when you know you are being looked at and judged. Now, *that* is scary. Nothing terrifies me more.

That's why I was so anxious when my teacher suggested that I take the audition for the American Ballet Theatre Company the following spring. I had already missed the school audition and knew the company would never consider me at my age, but the teacher insisted I go anyway. I said I had a doctor's appointment that day. I did have an appointment, but I could have cancelled it. The teacher told me in so many words I would be a complete fool if I passed up this opportunity. She thought I had potential that ought to be recognized immediately.

There were 314 people at the audition, standing around in an unfinished studio area. I was number 307. The dancers were all advanced, and I even recognized some of them as principal dancers from New Jersey companies. We filed into the studio and lined up for the first elimination.

The first elimination was on body type. Everyone stood in a line and was stared at. It was like a lineup in a beauty pageant. Those who were too small, too tall, muscular, overweight, or short-legged were left out when the numbers were called. I couldn't believe that as young as I looked, I was still there with eighty-seven others. The next part of the audition was a class.

Susan Jones, who was a soloist with American Ballet Theater, taught the class. I noticed that several of the judges kept leaning forward to see me. By this time, I was absolutely terrified. My knees felt mushy and I was perspiring a lot even though it was fairly cool I kept wondering what I was doing there. Everyone was sure to know as soon as we began the center floor exercises that I was nowhere near any of the others in skill level or technique or anything. Mr. Baryshnikov kept walking in and out of the room. I would then shrink further into my corner, not wanting to be seen. I figured if no one saw me, I couldn't be judged.

Probably only the exercise itself kept me from falling apart completely. By the time we got to center floor, I was not as nervous. Some of the older students were deliberately cutting me off when we did combinations across the floor, so I looked even worse. For the last part of the center floor we had to put on our pointe shoes. I couldn't believe I was still there. Barely keeping up, I finished the class. Before it was over, I managed to do one nice pirouette in front of Misha.

We waited in the loudest silence anyone could ever imagine. You could hear breathing all around and if you listened enough, probably heartbeats too. I never thought that I would be around after the last elimination. But I was still scared when they started to call the numbers of the ten finalists.

When they didn't call my number, I picked up my dance bag and started to leave the studio. But before I was all the way out the door, Mr. Baryshnikov called me to the front of the room.

I stood there with a new case of nervous shakes, as he asked my age and then told me I had to realize, of course, that I was too young for the company. Like an

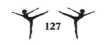

absolute fool, I replied that my teacher made me come to the audition. It was a stupid thing to say, but I really felt stupid being there.

But Mr. Baryshnikov smiled at me. He didn't seem at all put off by my silliness. He said I had potential and asked about my plans for the future. That was a question that was even easier to answer than my age. I told him I planned to be a ballerina someday and dance with a company like American Ballet Theatre. His reply amazed me. He asked if I would be interested in being in his special scholarship class. I didn't know what that was, but I knew it meant being very close to Ballet Theatre.

It took a while to realize what had happened to me at the audition. Nothing registered at all. There was Misha himself asking me to be part of a new program, an apprenticeship program. Later when it all hit me, I almost fell over.

Even though he had asked me, getting into the program was not quite that simple. Patricia Wilde, the director of the school, had just spent the better part of seven months traveling throughout the United States looking for students for the program. By the time I took the company audition, the summer group had already been chosen and there were no openings in the winter class.

Miss Wilde did agree to see me in one of her spring classes, with the possibility of putting me in the winter course if someone canceled. Everyone was better than I was, and I felt almost as intimidated as I had been during the company audition. I kept thinking I was in way over my head and needed perhaps another year or more at SAB to qualify. But even with the competition and the problems I had keeping up with the other students, I was told I could probably come for the summer but would have to wait for a decision on the winter course.

I had also taken the audition for SAB again. This time I had no ultimatums from Mom. In fact, I was asked to demonstrate the combination for the others during the audition, and I wasn't nervous a bit. The next thing I knew, I had to choose between the two schools. It was awful. I knew what it was like at SAB and I really loved it there. The program at American Ballet Theatre (ABT) was new, and I knew nothing about it except that Miss Lynn told me it was special training I wouldn't get anywhere else. I also knew people at SAB and didn't know anyone at ABT. It was one of the hardest choices of my life.

The fact that Baryshnikov himself had singled me out was the final reason. I decided to go to American Ballet Theatre School. The next thing I knew I was asked for a copy of my birth certificate, my most recent school grades, and three letters of recommendation from teachers. A scholarship form had to be filled out giving the details of my previous training.

My next problem was to find a place to live. Since I was only fourteen, my mother would not let me stay in the city alone, so I contacted the school registrar. Three out-of-state girls were also looking for a place, so we all got together and took a one-bedroom apartment hotel room. I was looking forward to my summer as an independent person. This was to be the beginning of a new life. At the age of fourteen, I was going to live in New York City and attend a full-time ballet school with the chance of staying on and maybe even getting into the company someday. It was a dream come true and it was just beginning. It was also the beginning of a lot of problems.

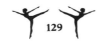

Summer and
Superstars

I moved into the city with great expectations. I met my new roommates and felt very grown up having my own apartment. The only problem was that one of the girl's mothers decided to have an extended vacation in New York and moved in with us for two weeks. This probably sounds mean of me, but this woman was really a typical ballet mother. She watched our every move and asked twenty questions about everything. The apartment was already overcrowded with four. We really didn't need her. I was also nervous because I was being considered for the winter class.

The summer group consisted of forty-five boys and girls from all over the United States. Some of them had already spent a year at American Ballet Theatre School. Others had been to the school the previous summer, and many of the rest were students from the School of American Ballet.

American Ballet Theatre had recently moved and was in a large building near Greenwich Village. Unfortunately, the move took place before the two floors Ballet Theatre had rented were completely renovated. The result was that in the middle of the studios were dirt piles, crowds of workmen, and loose debris of all kinds including glass, nails, and sawhorses. The girls' dressing room was plasterboard partitions. Often there were leering workmen in there as well. It was really a mess, and it also seemed dangerous. I had trouble imagining the place would ever be finished.

After two days, the school administration decided that the conditions were impossible, and they received permission to rent a studio upstairs at the famous 890 complex that shared space with Broadway play rehearsals. Unfortunately, summer is not the big season for Broadway, and nothing more exciting than a television commercial was filmed there.

Every week a different famous person from American Ballet Theatre company taught our classes in addition to the regular teachers. Included on the list were Michael Lland and Susan Jones, who were a ballet master and mistress who taught the company dancers. The dancers who worked with us were George de la Pena, Cynthia Gregory, Charlie Maple, Hilda Morales, Rebecca Wright, Christine Spizzo, and Johan Renvall. Every one of them had a definite style of teaching and we were all inspired to do our best.

The highlight of the session was Cynthia Gregory. She taught us the White Swan Variation from *Swan Lake* in our pointe and variations class. All the posters and famous pictures of Cynthia have her posed in that role and she is so beautiful even in rehearsal clothes. At the end of class we presented her with a dozen red roses and she took bows. I found out later that this was the first time she had ever taught a class and she was actually nervous!

Life was like a big party for the first few weeks. Then my roommates discovered that I might be accepted for the winter program. They might as well have found out I had leprosy. Suddenly, I found myself in a subtly armed fortress. At first, it was a few nasty remarks; then it was all-out war.

One of the girls was fairly nice, but we had the usual problems of too many people living together. We fought over who would do the dishes, and the apartment was always a mess with clothes strewn all over and ballet stuff hanging everywhere. One of the girls ate most of the food I bought and called me anorexic (which is someone who is too skinny and starves on purpose). Another one said I would never be a dancer because I would get fat and ugly. I just couldn't win.

I had always been skinny, but never anorectic. Some girls in ballet have anorexia nervosa, because someone is always after them about being too fat. What happens is the girl goes on a diet and loses some weight. Then everyone compliments her, so she loses more and more and finally she looks like she is a skeleton. It's really scary to see someone like that. Some girls are even more extreme. They go on big eating binges and then feel guilty, thinking they will gain lots of weight, so they make themselves throw up. No matter how skinny these girls get, they always complain about being too fat. It is a very weird disease that I hope I never get. I seem to stay thin no matter how much I eat. But I am also still growing and my body could change.

I can always tell when I start to grow. My center of balance somehow shifts, and I have trouble with pirouettes. It seems like I am always relearning how to place my body to balance properly.

After the trouble with my roommates began, I made friends with Eliska, a California girl who was already selected for the winter program. Whenever the fights with the roommates began, I would phone Ellie, trying to make myself feel better.

I didn't know it at the time, but one of the other girls selected for the winter program had given up her position. With an opening available, another girl and I were being considered. Every class became like an audition, and I was a lot younger and weaker than my competitor.

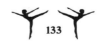

I never did like competitive activities. When I was younger, I was on a swim team. I really didn't like getting cold and wet. I guess the reason was I just was not into sports, especially outdoor sports. I was not the worst one on the swim team, but I was certainly not very good. My heart was just not in it. I guess I always knew I wanted to be a ballerina. I like the kind of competition that goes with dance because you are really competing with yourself. The pressure is just as bad—probably worse—but it is a challenge I like. (Even when I end up crying half the time.)

Our summer schedule was very tiring, with two to three classes per day six days a week. Partnering (pas de deux) classes were particularly interesting because I didn't have many of them before. These classes were

Scott was my pas de deux partner.

taught by Charlie Maple and George de la Pena. Charlie was teaching us the pas de deux from *Le Corsaire* (the slave). It is an exciting dance with very difficult steps and big lifts done by the boys. The poor boys were having their own trouble trying to lift us. Few of them had the strength to do anything beyond a half lift. Because I was young and light, I was usually paired with one of the younger boys. It was like the blind leading the blind. We were both usually frustrated half to death.

George de la Pena had starred in the movie *Nijinsky*, and it was really neat being taught by a movie star who was also a fine dancer. His pas de deux classes were more basic, with fewer fancy lifts. He also put us in lines, and we constantly changed partners, so I wasn't as frustrated. George had us do some of the simple partnering moves like waltzes. He was a very exacting teacher and expected no nonsense, whereas Charlie tried to make the class more fun. We learned a lot from both of them, and those of us who stayed on through the winter were to do the *Corsaire* pas de deux until we knew it backwards.

Hilda Morales worked primarily with the girls. In addition to being a company ballet mistress, she was also one of the soloists. During our classes, she wore a long flowing dress and inspired us to break away from stiff formal exercises and move.

We had some interesting people taking classes with us. When the Royal Ballet was in the city, many of their dancers came in. The same thing happened with La Scala, the Italian opera company. We never knew what to expect. I think that was what made the summer so exciting.

When Johan Renvall taught class, half the girls fell in love with him. He is a gorgeously handsome

Swedish artist who dances like the wind and jumps high and effortlessly like a gazelle. His big green eyes would melt us, as he explained what he wanted us to do, and we would all try our best. Even the boys were envious of Johan's jumps. He seemed to stay in the air forever.

Studying with Susan Jones and Michael Lland was like taking a company class. Susan had taught the class for the company audition. We had so many differnt styles taught to us. Rebecca Wright and Chris Spizzo were very technical. They were also both very nice.

When Johan taught class, we fell in love with him.

Sometime near the middle of the session, I was informed officially that I was being considered for the winter program. The letter contained a special medical form designed for dance students with questions like, "What is the degree of turnout?" and "length of toes": things one would never find on an ordinary medical form. It was hard to find a doctor who even understood the meaning of some of the requests. One girl said her doctor had to call the ballet school and ask for an explanation. We had to have our hip sockets rotated, our feet examined for any unusual growths like bunions, our knees flexed and straightened for signs of hyperextension (which looks like a bowed leg from the side view), and our spines examined for straightness. We even had our legs measured to see if they were the same length. All these things could cause problems, and some of them could become serious medical handicaps as we grew older.

I was also advised to apply for entrance to the Professional Children's School, as the class schedule at Ballet Theatre School was to be full time, lasting from 10:30 A.M. to 5:30 P.M. Several places had been held at the school for the students selected for the ballet program. My friend Ellie was already enrolled. If I was accepted into the winter dance session, I would be on correspondence most of the time. A student on correspondence has a much more difficult time than one who attends classes. It takes hard work to keep up with the assignments. Fortunately, I had always been a good student. I guess I carried the discipline of dance into my schoolwork.

As I received more and more information on the winter program of ABT school, life became unbearable with my three roommates. I often spent the night with Ellie. I finally called my mother and asked if I

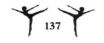

I was advised to apply to Professional Children's School, as were many of my other dancer friends.

could move in with Ellie. Since the rent was already paid, Mom talked me into staying where I was. She also had a very long talk with my roommates, and somehow the fighting stopped. Ellie and I went sightseeing with the little free time we had. Even though I had been to New York City many times when I lived in New Jersey, it was fun showing it to Ellie. We shopped at Macy's and in Greenwich Village and went to movies on the Upper West Side, which is where Lincoln Center is located. There isn't much going on in the center during the summer, but we still had fun exploring.

Sometimes Ellie would go home with me to New Jersey for the weekend. Whenever I brought someone there for the first time, the person made me feel like I lived in a mansion. We have a twenty-acre farm with five cows, seven chickens, and five horses. The cows are to butcher, the chickens are for eggs, and the horses are for breeding. I used to ride them, but I lost interest. That was another competitive sport I tried for a while.

Unlike my trials with swimming, I took well to horseback riding. I learned all the basics of equitation and eventually took up jumping. This can be extremely difficult. It is very easy to fall off or, worse, go over the hurdle without the horse. I saw it happen lots of times. Sometimes riders can really get hurt. I only competed in one horse show, but I won second place in the jumping class.

Horseback riding is lots of fun, but it is terrible if you study ballet because it works all the wrong muscles. So I gave up riding, which was one of the few outside activities I had. Now I don't have any hobbies except going to movies or shopping or going to parties. I just don't have the time or energy. I wish I could say I did needlepoint or something, but I don't. However, I do plan to take up knitting someday. It's a great way to save money on leg warmers.

That summer, I went home about every third weekend. By late July the weather in New York City had become unbearably hot. Fortunately, the ABT studio was air-conditioned. Even so, the energy level was very low. No one felt like eating and we drank enormous amounts of soda.

Members of the artistic staff were returning to reorganize the company for its winter season, and among them was Baryshnikov. Several of the girls and I were determined to have him autograph a photo. We spent all our spare time making up dumb reasons to hang around the administrator's desk because he always walked by there. It seemed that as soon as we left for class, he would appear. I got tired of playing games, so finally I asked where his office was and walked down there. When I think back, I can't believe I did such a nervy thing. I do remember my knees shaking when I asked him to sign the picture. But he was nice to me.

Since I was likely to be accepted into the winter program, my parents had begun to make preparations for me to stay in the city. They got me an apartment in a nice area off Fifth Avenue. They were going to let me live there with Ellie and her older sister. I was lucky to never have had a bad experience in New York. I guess it was because I felt I had lived there all my life. My home life was much more sheltered on the farm, but I was also what is called street wise. Street wise is being able to spot trouble before it sees you and avoid it. I had no desire to drink or experiment with drugs like some kids my age. I had already seen a close friend of mine become an addict.

It was great having my own apartment.

The destruction of that person's life was so terrible it made me never want to try drugs.

Ballet is a strange world. You have to really be on the ball to do well and progress. It takes a maturity that most young people do not want to deal with. You leave home at a much younger age than most kids and have to learn how to be on your own. And you have to deal with an adult life-style. It's like going away to college at the age of fourteen or fifteen. Lots of kids are just not ready for it—I'm not so sure I was either.

As the end of August and the last of the summer program were near, the weather became hotter and classes became more difficult. By this time, I knew the complete *Corsair* pas de deux and several interest-

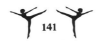

Shane Gregory and I became good friends at Professional Children's School.

ing variations. People who had once been larger-than-life superstars to most of us were now our friends. I still had not heard about the winter course. Then the miracle occurred. The other girl being considered for the program decided not to stay in New York. Actually, her mother decided for her. The girl had one more year of high school, and she decided to finish before settling in the East.

Right after that, another girl already chosen for the program arrived early and was taken directly into the first company. It looked like I was in the school with no more wondering or suspense.

142

The winter course looked extremely exciting. Not only would I be taking classes in classical ballet but I would learn other dance forms such as modern and character (folk dance). We were also going to have some nondancing classes like art history and dance notation. It was going to be a school like no other ballet school. We were to be trained with the idea of apprenticing us into the company. It was going to be a year like no other in my life.

They also finished the studios downstairs. The place looked every bit as wonderful as the School of American Ballet. We would share the space with the companies of ABT and ABT II. ABT II held a summer workshop the last two weeks of our summer course and two of my summer roommates were asked to participate. Once the word was out that I was in the winter program, the girls became snobbish again. I had lots of trouble being liked when I was successful. I tried not to seem nose-in-the-air about the whole thing, but I guess I came off that way. What can I say? I have been extremely lucky and I'm not going to crawl away and hide because of it. Of course, it hasn't been all luck. Most of it has been very hard work. As they say, success has its price. All I hope for is to be really successful, to make it to the top. I think I have a good chance if I don't get injured or fat or something.

When the summer session was over, my roommates and I parted friends. We wished each other luck, and they set out to continue their lives in their hometowns. I couldn't wait for the first day of my new classes. It was also the first day of the most frustrating year of my life.

The Child of Ballet
Theatre

September 8, 1981, was the day after Labor Day. It was also the first day of the experimental program at Ballet Theatre School, and there I was the youngest—at fourteen—in a group of twelve. Lots of people called us the dirty dozen. We didn't know what to call ourselves, but we knew were were lucky.

Ballet Theatre School had gone from a student body of five-hundred kids and adults to forty to the twelve of us in only three years time. The school was thirty years old. As privileged as we were, we sure didn't look like much. Some of us were terrified of being left alone in New York City. Others had been in the group the year before.

I had a lot of my own trouble. Besides my age, I was at a disadvantage because several of the others knew Misha had singled me out at the company audition. Sometimes I heard comments like, "She's got it made. After all, she's Misha's little pet."

Since none of us were used to wearing a uniform, almost everyone ignored the printed dress code and showed up in ratty clothes. The girls spent extra time in the dressing room arranging their hair into fancy braided buns, and sometimes all this fussing made us late for classes. We were told once that our messy clothes and fancy hair made us look like a bunch of well-combed ragpickers. The boys didn't fuss with their hair, but they were just as bad with their clown-like costumes.

The first week was a trial for everyone. We wanted to prove we deserved to be there, and the instructors tried to like us even though we were a mess. Our first official roast was after Misha looked in at us the second or third day and saw our strange outfits. We were told to follow the dress code or else. I was scared that

Misha would notice me and see how much worse I was than the others and send an order to have me thrown out. Everyone called me his pet, but I was afraid of being the first failure. Most of the time during that week I was close to tears.

The studios were finished enough to allow classes to be given in the same area with the company. Sometimes we couldn't hear the instructors because a drill was running. Badly attached barres fell off the walls into our hands and the windows wouldn't open because they had been painted shut. On cool days, the air-conditioning would turn on, and when the weather was warm, the heat would kick in. Pipes sometimes burst and flooded the studio floor. Newly painted walls never had "wet paint signs," so we often had white splotches on our leotards. The floors were filthy from plaster dust and shavings.

Valentina Vishnevsky, a very sweet Russian lady who was our accompanist, would come in early and have to remove food wrappers, empty juice cartons, and cigarette butts from the top of the piano so she could set up her music. It was difficult for all of us, but somehow we managed three full classes a day. Most of us were not used to so much work. We came in each morning more and more exhausted and with extremely sore and weak muscles. I had absolutely no energy at all. It was all I could do to get out of bed in the morning. At night I was too tired to fix anything to eat. My typical lunch was a bologna sandwich and some instant pudding. I washed it down with soda. If Mom had known what I was eating, she probably would have killed me—or at least taken me home.

But even with all the problems, I would not have traded my life with anyone. The first company was already beginning rehearsals for the fall season and I couldn't believe seeing so many familiar faces all at once. The summer course had been exciting with a lot of famous dancers, but having them all there at the same time was just too much. I would be sitting in the lounge eating my sandwich, and Leslie Browne would walk by or Misha would stop and buy a soda from the machine. It was as if I were suddenly picked up and put right in the middle of *The Turning Point*, but instead of a movie, it was real.

We had other kinds of excitement too. One of the classes that set us apart from the other ballet schools was art history. Once a week during our lunch break, we would listen to a lecture on art and how it related to dance. Also once a week, we took a field trip to one of the large art museums in the city. One of the most exciting trips was to the Cloisters museum following our lecture on medieval art.

The Cloisters is a large medieval museum constructed from old buildings that were brought over from Europe stone by stone. It is part of the Metropolitan Museum of Art, but is at the other end of Manhattan. We had to take a long subway ride to get there. We got the whole morning off for the trip. When we stepped out of the subway station, we saw the most perfect October day imaginable. The leaves had begun to turn fall colors and we felt so free and wonderful that we started skipping through the park. Some of us even sang. It was hard to believe we were still in Manhattan. The park was like a scene from the *Sound of Music*, with green lawns and high cliffs in the distance. We later learned that the cliffs were called the Palisades. When we saw the Cloisters in the distance, it was like being in Europe and seeing a castle rise up from behind a hill. It looked like a fortress, the kind with a moat and everything.

They had arranged a guided tour for us that lasted over two and a half hours. Our tour guide was very nice. She told us all about medieval life among the monks and then took us to the room with the famous unicorn tapestries. We sat on the floor while she pointed out all the symbols and told us their meanings. She explained how the unicorn was thought to represent Christ and the virgin was the Virgin Mary. One of the tapestries was kind of gruesome. It showed the unicorn being stabbed by lots of hunters. The one I liked showed the unicorn lying down in a little fenced yard. It was supposed to represent paradise.

After seeing the tapestries, the guide took us out to the herb gardens and explained that everything growing there was raised in medieval times. The herbs smelled good and we were all getting hungry, so we left the Cloisters to have lunch at a nearby cafeteria.

The cafeteria was in a grove of trees in the park. I felt like we were eating at a country inn. It had an outdoor patio and we sat under trees that were filled with songbirds. It was really nice to get out of the "city." The relaxed atmosphere brought us all a little closer together that day. We had begun a few weeks before as individuals after our own goals; suddenly we were becoming a kind of artistic family. I think the Cloisters trip was our true beginning as a group.

We went back to the studio that afternoon to take the modern dance class. I hated the class because I just couldn't dance like that. All our movements were into weird angles and almost everything we did was the opposite of ballet. My head-rolls had corners on them and my hips would not swing. Nothing seemed to move the way it was supposed to. It was not fun for me at all. The only good thing was that it was just once a week. It was in the modern dance class that I had my first mishap. We were doing an extreme plié movement where we moved sharply from one foot to the other with our knees bent, when something seemed to give out in one knee. As soon as I realized I had hurt myself, I panicked. I thought I was ruined. Knee injuries can be the worst. Sometimes your knees are never right again. I began to cry and limped out of the studio. Ellie ran and got me an ice pack and I was put on a chair with one leg propped up. I couldn't stop crying, and I soon realized that there was a whole crowd of dancers around me including many of the company members. I remember Leslie Browne patting me on the shoulder and saying I would be okay. Someone else called a doctor. I kept crying, thinking it was the end of my whole dance career.

I guess I have a tendency to overreact, because the doctor told me it was only a strain and said to wrap the knee and not dance for a couple of days. That was it. My career wasn't ruined or anything. I went home for the weekend to calm down and pull myself together.

During the summer, I had spent most of my weekends in New Jersey, but once fall began, I only went home every third weekend. Besides my family, the thing I missed most was my dog, Ippy. She is a rare breed of Chinese dog called a shar-pei. Most people think they are very weird-looking because they have such loose skin. They have lots and lots of big wrinkles and the more wrinkles on them, the more valuable they are. Some puppies are worth as much as $4,000.

My family first became interested in them after my dad took a business trip to China and brought back some pictures. We bought the first puppy in the United States. Our second and third ones came from China.

They really are funny dogs. They snore at night. I guess it's because of their short noses, which are like bulldogs', only much cuter. Most of the dogs grow to be almost forty pounds and they are very lovable. One of our dogs had three puppies, two black and one fawn-colored. We had to give two of them to the breeder but we kept one of the black ones and named him Magoo. Mom thought it would be a good idea to try to breed the dogs because they are so rare. I just love having them around as pets. I wished I could keep Ippy in my New York apartment, but I had to settle for lots of pictures in my wallet like a proud parent with pictures of her kids.

At first, I was really torn between the city and the country. I wanted all the advantages of living in New York with all the comforts of home like having my dog around and Mom cooking wonderful meals. The New Jersey farm also has a hot tub, something I really could use after a hard day of classes. That warm water was good therapy for my injured knee.

After my injury I couldn't wait to finish with modern classes and start something else. We were supposed to have only six weeks of modern, and I hoped it was true. I was weak in ballet and wanted to concentrate on getting stronger. I didn't want to add any injury to my weakness. My worst problems were in pas de deux class. It seemed no matter how hard I worked, I couldn't get the combination right. The situation just kept getting worse. The more I tried, the more tense I became, until I couldn't do anything well at all. I knew I was awful, and I was also certain that John Prinz, our instructor, hated me. I'm sure he thought everything he said went out my other ear because I just kept doing worse. One day he seemed particularly angry, and I ran out of the studio into the dressing room. He hated it when any of us cried, so I wouldn't show my frustration in front of him. But the tears came quickly once I was in the dressing room. I didn't know what to do. Everything was wrong and I couldn't make it better. My feet were still very weak on toe and I was all off balance.

If that wasn't enough, I also had a terrible time getting things right in my character class. Character dancing is like folk dancing. Ballet dancers have to learn it for many of the roles in the classical ballets, since most of these ballets are stories about princesses in foreign countries. Character dances have very sharp movements like a quick twist of the hand or a series of small complicated jumps. I thought I was going to go crazy learning so much at once. I was always tired and I'm sure that didn't help, either.

But at least I liked the character classes. The music was fun, especially in this one gypsy dance we learned. We were flying all over the studio. I remember one time when a girl in the class got so carried away she accidentally hit a boy in the face. It's a wonder I didn't do the same thing to some of my partners. We learned a dance called the mazurka, which is a wild Polish dance, and a more elegant dance called the czardas, which is very hard on the leg muscles because of its slowness. We also learned a Spanish dance and a Russian dance. Later we were to perform all of these dances for an audience.

Our performance skills were perfected in a class we had once a week called workshop. This involved learning dances for lecture demonstrations that were held in schools in the New York City area. Mr. Prinz would talk and then we would show the students some of the steps used in a ballet class. After the short class, some of us would perform dances from the different ballets. This was usually done in full costume. We borrowed the costumes from the company. We loved wearing them because the tutus were made out of real velvet and had all kinds of beautiful glass jewels on them.

Only the better students got to perform in the lecture demonstrations and the rest of us had to understudy them. I learned everything, but was still weak and clumsy, so I figured I would never be chosen to do anything. There were reasons that the same people always got to do the performances. Our school director, Patricia Wilde, wanted to show our group in the best possible way. We were still experimental, and we wanted to show the rest of the ballet schools that we were special. Therefore, only the most talented of us got to be in the spotlight. We also had to rent a van to get to the performances. Only a certain number of people could fit inside with the costumes and the portable barres.

Our programs were such a success that calls kept coming in asking us to perform. I was determined to participate in one of these shows before the year was

Our performance skills were perfected in a workshop class.

over, and I worked hard learning every role. The one I wanted to do the most was the *Corsair* pas de deux. It is by far the most beautiful and romantic of the selections our group learned. But Lisa did that one the best. Her movements extended beyond the end of her fingers. Lisa *was* Corsair. Compared with her, I looked like a piece of stiff cardboard with a frightened red face from working so hard.

When we weren't totally exhausted, Ellie and I went to the movies on weekends. Sometimes we were joined by a few of the older scholarship students such as Ted, Jeff, and Anna. When we had extra money, we would go into the restaurants on Columbus Avenue and people-watch. Columbus Avenue is a street on the Upper West Side near Lincoln Center. It is one of the nicer streets of New York City and it's active almost all night long. Several of the boys in our class worked extra hours at an ice cream shop in that area, so we would get lots of free cones when we stopped by to say hello. This was really our whole social life.

I didn't have time to have a boyfriend. I was too tired most of the time to be interested in boys anyway. The only thing I wanted to talk about or think about was dance, and no one but another dancer would find that very interesting. Most of the boys who danced were like us, too busy or too exhausted to think about dating. The kids in our classes were all good friends. I guess I was lucky because we weren't under the kind of pressure most high school kids face when they date. We would go to movies and work on ballet combinations together, but we weren't thinking of romance. Maybe I was just too young to recognize it anyway. All I wanted to do was improve my dancing and keep from being injured.

Another important class developed because of the injuries. Almost everyone had problems with knees, ankles, backs, or feet. Each one of us had a bad something or other, so a class was added called kineotherapy. This was anatomy for the dancer and how to avoid injury. The instructor looked at each of us individually during class and analyzed what we were doing wrong that caused strain. My fault was bad posture. Because I was growing so quickly, my weight center was not in the right place and I was working the wrong muscles. This kind of thing is called bad placement, and if it is not corrected, it can cause all kinds of terrible problems. I began to see a chiropractor in addition to taking anatomy classes. We also learned more about our bodies and the limits we could push them to. Too many dancers think if it doesn't hurt, it isn't doing any good. Then once they are injured, they are afraid of losing strength, so they don't give themselves time to heal and sometimes go as far as to perform on a broken foot or sprained ankle. Some dancers even take classes and rehearse in casts and on crutches!

The first two months we worked hard and complained all the time about having too many classes and being exhuasted. Then all of a sudden, we had an incredible amount of energy. Many students would find an empty studio after classes and work on their own. I usually had too much homework for that. My school day consisted of two early morning classes. I would be at the studio by 10 A.M. Because I was on correspondence, I was pretty much on my own to get the work done on time and be prepared for the tests. Every so often I would have a conference with a teacher on my progress. It's hard to work on your own, and I was usually way behind. When I was due to take a test, I would panic. My worst subject was French, because what I learned was only from a book and from tapes and I didn't have any real opportunity to use the language in a classroom. This made it very confusing to me. My other bad class was geography. I almost failed the final exam. One of the things that saved me was borrowing notes from a boy who took the regular geography class. His name was Shane Gregory, and he was in my homeroom. Another girl told me he was the best student in the class, so I asked if he could loan me his notes to study. They helped clear up some of the confusing parts of the book. No one could help me in French. I was in tears during that exam. Professional Children's School is much more difficult than other schools, primarily because those who have heavy work schedules are expected to know as much as those who attend classes much of the time. I know very few kids — no matter how mature they are or how smart—who can keep up. The secret is to schedule your most difficult classes when you can attend them, but it doesn't always work out.

All in all, I was having problems, but I was also afraid that Mom might think it was a mistake to let me stay on my own in New York. I knew I had a lot to prove. I had to convince my instructors at Ballet Theatre that I could keep up with the older students. I had to show my teachers at Professional Children's School that I could pass the courses. And I had to prove to myself that I truly did have what it takes to be a success.

Long Ride on a
Merry-Go-Round

I always loved vacations. We got two weeks off from ABT for Christmas and most of the kids went home. Before everyone left, we had a tree-trimming party at Shane's house that was really fun. We spent over two hours decorating a gigantic fir tree. After we put the tree up, we stepped back to admire our work. Suddenly, the tree started to lean forward and fell on the coffee table right into the onion dip and everything! We had to rope it to the wall before we put back all the decorations. Amazingly, only one ornament broke. I met Shane's sister, Stephanie, for the first time. She was a ringer for my best friend. I even showed her pictures and Stephanie agreed she looked like my friend.

I now had lots of good friends, especially among the other scholarship students. All the little jealousies and big ego problems had given way to our common goal. We all wanted to be in the first company of ABT, and most of us were afraid it would never happen. Our program had been running since September, and Misha had only looked in on us a few times. Except for being told to wear uniforms, we didn't get any feedback on how we were doing. The company had been on tour much of that time, so we figured once they were back for their season at the Met, we would learn a lot more.

After the first of the year, a new modern class began with a different teacher. She had been trained in ballet and seemed to know more about our movement problems. But when I first heard we were going to have another modern class, I thought I would die. I thought, why couldn't we have jazz or music theory or any of the other classes that were suggested? But once we began, I felt more comfortable. The teacher was patient with me and didn't expect too much. I didn't realize it at the time, but the other modern class did give me a start on this movement form that made it much easier to pick up the second time. The new teacher also had a very inspiring accompanist. His music made you want to dance. I discovered the reason we didn't have other kinds of dance classes was because Patricia Wilde wanted us to master one dance form before going on to another. She thought if we had both jazz and modern, it would be too confusing.

We did get other opportunities, however. The school got lots of calls from casting directors, movie producers, and famous photographers. They were looking for young dancers for commericals, films, and dancewear ads. But every time someone came to look at us, I was either too old or too young. Some of the others got to go in and audition and almost everyone was interested in Ellie. She had already done an important role in the movie, *Pennies from Heaven*, and had one of those faces everyone wanted to photograph. But Ellie didn't want to be in films. Like me, all she wanted to do was dance, so she usually refused the offers.

I did get in on one of the outside calls. The incredible artistic photographer, Harvey Edwards, came to the studio one day looking for a model and picked Lisa. After she did some work for him, he sent another representative to get some more models for a Freeds ad. Freeds is a famous British dancewear manufacturer that advertises in all the major dance magazines. Four of us got to go and do the photo session: me, Courtney, Ellie, and another girl from the second company named Linda. I got the job because Anna had been asked to go and had to cancel at the last minute.

We were picked up in a limousine around ten in the morning and driven to a waterfront house on Long Island. I got to wear a pink unitard. We posed in various stretching positions most of the morning. We had a break around noon and lunch was brought in for us. Harvey came in after lunch and watched the next session. He was really funny and kept telling us jokes while we worked. When we were done, he had his own limousine take us home. The driver not only took us back to Manhattan to our apartments but he took Courtney all the way home to New Jersey. I felt like a celebrity.

I was still having trouble with my schoolwork, but things were starting to pick up for me in my ballet classes. Mr. Prinz and his wife, Nanette, were asked to find five girls for a performance at Town Hall. They picked Courtney, Anna, Mary, and Ellie, with Lisa dancing the lead role with Doug. The dance was a piece that had originally been choreographed by Balanchine. It was called *Valse Fantasy*, and the costumes were the originals, borrowed from New York City Ballet. Everyone wanted to be in the performance because it was a very beautiful classical dance and even the corps members were in constant dancing motion. It was fun and light and very romantic. I was asked to understudy Anna. I was very disappointed at first because I knew Anna would dance on a broken leg if she had to. This was her favorite dance.

Halfway through rehearsals, however, I got my big chance. Lisa began to have problems with her foot and couldn't dance on toe without horrible pain. Since Anna was the understudy for the lead role, she began to take over for Lisa. This left Anna's corps part for me. No one was certain what would happen by the time we had to perform. Lisa would seem to improve and then her foot would begin to hurt again. We kept rehearsing and changing around in the roles. Someone came over from City Ballet to help stage the piece and see that the choreography was correct. Lisa was still unable to dance full out, so Anna was officially given the lead and I was in for the performance!

Then I almost blew it. With this woman from City Ballet watching us, I was trying too hard. One section of the studio floor was very slippery, and when I did a high kick, my standing foot went out from under me and I fell smack on my lower back.

I was terrified. I didn't know what horrible thing I had done to myself. It felt like I had broken something, and movement was very painful. Here we were only a week and a half from performance, I had my first chance to show what I could do, and I went and fell on my back. I was absolutely panic-stricken.

That evening I went to the chiropractor and he said I just had a bad bruise on my tailbone. By the first of the next week I was dancing again. I felt sorry for Lisa because I knew what she was going through watching Anna do her role. Injuries are the most maddening thing in a dancer's life, because you never know how far you can push yourself.

I was both excited and nervous the night of the performance. I put on my costume and stood before the mirror. This performance was the beginning for me. It wasn't the Met, but it was a stage, and an audience would be there to see me as a ballerina in a tutu and pointe shoes. My future was beginning (at least I hoped it was).

The stage was extremely small and we had trouble fitting the choreography in the tiny space, but we got

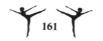

through the performance without an obvious mistake and everyone seemed to love us. I did so well that I was given another opportunity to dance.

ABT School was asked to do another lecture demonstration at a large fancy private school in Manhattan. I not only got to do *Valse Fantasy* again, but I also did the demonstration at the barre. We were going to have a class at the school as well as a full rehearsal before the performance. The dressing room was under the stage. We had a lighted mirror and a long counter top where we put all our junk. Some of the older girls smoked, something I hope never to do. I know a lot of the girls who smoke would like to stop but they can't. They say it helps break nervous tension. Most of my tension is usually held inside. That's probably why I cry so easily when things go wrong.

I wasn't on until the last dance, so I had lots of time to do my makeup and hair. One thing dancers learn early is how to do their own makeup. Even boys learn how to handle eyeliner and pancake foundation. If they didn't wear eyeliner, it would look as if they didn't have any eyes under the harsh stage lighting.

During this performance, *Valse Fantasy* was even better than it had been at Town Hall. It was a very special moment for Anna. Unfortunately, that afternoon Anna sprained her ankle. I don't know why it is, but it seems that whenever a dancer crosses a barrier and does something particularly special, something like an injury happens to set the person back. It has happened to everyone I know.

But even with all the mishaps, we were asked back for a second lecture demonstration for the older students. This particular performance was to take place the week before Easter. Unfortunately, it was also the second day of the worst snowstorm in New York City that year. The snow had been so bad the day before that the school had been closed. If we had been asked to perform that day, we would have all been out of luck.

This was probably the most important lecture demonstration we had done so far. The first company was back in New York City and rumor had it that Misha was going to come and watch us. This was very likely the most he would ever see of us, and we had to be at our best.

Since the performance was in the city and the school didn't have to rent a van, the entire class was allowed to participate in one or more pieces. I was supposed to do the barre demonstration, a modern combination, and the character dances. None of my parts were solo. I would always be with the group, but that didn't make me any less scared.

While we rehearsed, the storm became wilder. We were worried that the school might be closed the next morning and we would be canceled.

We all hoped the performance would go as well as the rehearsal had. The only thing that bummed me out was after we did the modern piece I was cut. Several people said I didn't fit in at all and it would make me look bad if I performed it.

The snow raged on and we trudged out to catch taxis home, still not knowing what to expect the next morning. I went out to dinner with Ellie, Jeff, and Ted, and we talked only about what might happen. Ted was hoping for a contract. He had been practicing every day in empty studios to improve his jumps. Of all the boys, Ted was definitely the best jumper. He looked like he was being held up in the air because he was so light on his feet and went up so high.

We were all worried not just about what would happen to us but what would happen to the program in general. It was already April and no one seemed to know what plans were in store for the school. The director and administrator were waiting for word from the artistic staff. The program had been so difficult and specialized that everyone in it was wondering what it was all for. Everyone did agree we were getting great training and more classes than any other program in the city. We knew we were very lucky to have had what we did, no matter what became of the school. People from all over the world were trying to get in every day and were turned away.

The next morning it was still snowing, but we went to the school theater praying it would be open. It was. We had heard that many of the New York City

Rehearsals were always strenuous.

Schools were closed, but luckily this was not one of them. The performance was on.

My hand shook as I put on my eye makeup. Someone had seen Misha. I wished I had more to do in the performance, but, on the other hand, it would give me more to mess up. Being cut from the modern section was probably a good thing. All I needed was for Misha to see how awkward I was with those movements.

When we got onstage, I thought I saw Misha in the balcony. I smiled and gave it everything I had during the barre and center floor demonstrations. I was terrified and my knees felt like rubber bands, but I did all right and didn't make any glaring mistakes. When we got back to the dressing room, some of the other girls were in tears. It was one of the few times I wasn't crying too. I had a lot more confidence when we went back out for the character dances.

Afterward, Mary and I went to a nearby pizza place for lunch. When we walked in, I almost died. Misha was there with Terry Orr. I wanted to turn right around and leave, but it was too late. They saw us. When Misha said we had done very well, Mary and I almost fainted. We sat near them, and Terry asked us lots of questions about how we liked the program and what our future plans were and how long we had studied. We kept talking while Misha leaned his chin on his hand and listened. I hardly even remember what I said. I only remember seeing Misha watching us and wondering what he was thinking. Did he like me? Did he still think I was worth keeping around? There were so many questions I wanted to ask, but I was afraid to even look at him for too long for fear he might disappear. After they left, Mary and I looked at each other with the same expression. I knew she also wondered what our fate was going to be.

The Apprentice

When the first company began its season at the Metropolitan Opera House, they put up a notice at the school that they needed supers for some of their full-length ballets like *Giselle, Swan Lake,* and *Don Quixote.* "Super" is short for supernumerary, which is someone with a small, nondancing part. Instead of using the company's trained members, it is easier to pay five dollars a performance to extras. This also gives the students a chance to work with the company and see what it is like being onstage in the Met.

We were all excited about the audition for supers. One morning before class a representative from the company had us go to the large studio. What I didn't realize then was that they pick supers not on ability, but on height and whether or not the people fit the costumes. I was not the right size and was not chosen for any of the ballets. I was awfully disappointed. I was looking forward to seeing what it was like backstage at the Met, and after the audition I didn't think I would get another chance.

But I guess I overreact to everything, because in less than a week I did get the opportunity to be onstage. The company was staging a new ballet called *Great Galloping Gottschalk,* and they needed people to wear the costumes and stand onstage so they could practice with the lighting. Since I didn't get the super job, I was asked to go to the staging.

It turned out that I was wearing Hilda Morales's costume. It was a weird-looking thing with a skirt and pants. My hair had been done with little fans stuck in it. Some of the people there said I looked like Darcy Kistler, who is the beautiful new star at New York City Ballet. Wow, if I could begin my career like she did at sixteen, I would feel like the luckiest girl in the

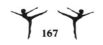

world. No one could have given me a more wonderful compliment.

I was very impressed with the Met stage. It is both wide and deep. It was so different from the stages in high school auditoriums where I performed in the *Nutcracker*. Everything was bigger and better. The neatest thing was looking out into the audience from the stage. The balconies went back and back and back for what seemed like a mile. I couldn't even imagine what it would look like with people in all those seats.

But I had my chance to see an audience too. Three weeks after the *Gottschalk* staging, one of the *Swan Lake* supers couldn't make a performance. And in my usual understudy way, I got to go on for her. I went in that evening to try on the costume and realized at once why I wasn't chosen in the first place. It was huge, and it had been pinned way up for the other girl. They did everything but cut it up to make it presentable for me. Even then I was practically falling out of the monstrous dress. It was heavy too. The material looked and felt like it was made from carpets. I was supposed to look like an aristocrat, but I looked more like a little kid playing dress-up.

Since all I had to do was follow some of the other supers on stage and sit, there was no need for a rehearsal. That evening we took our places while the curtain was still down and waited for the second act to begin. Even more exciting than being there was seeing Cynthia Gregory dance the role of the Black Swan. One of the things that surprised me was how much talking and giggling goes on between the dances. We were supposed to be royalty commenting on the party, but the conversation was more teasing than anything.

I was very impressed with the dressing rooms at the Met. They had individual closets and lighted mirrors. There were lots and lots of sinks and even showers. It was like a minimansion, and, in a way, I guess I did feel like royalty. As things turned out, I was a substitute super in a number of performances. I got a backstage pass and was able to see other ballets from the wings.

When I wasn't backstage or onstage, I worked for the boutique. The boutique is a little area in the upstairs lobby that sells T-shirts, posters, buttons, and jewelry. Some of us were offered the opportunity to work for the boutique, and instead of getting pay, we would get free tickets for the performances. We would find out the program the day before, and if it was something or someone we especially wanted to see, we would volunteer.

One night Ellie and I sold buttons. We walked all around with baskets. I looked down from the third balcony and saw Peter Martins in the first-floor lobby. We ran down the stairs, bumping into people to get to him before he disappeared. I was very nervous and giggled a lot when I asked him if he would like to buy a button. My face was probably bright red from blushing. I guess he felt sorry for me, because he bought a button. It's funny when I think about it— selling a Ballet Theatre button to a principal dancer from New York City Ballet.

With all the evening performances, my schoolwork was suffering. I was getting way behind in my French, and it looked like I would either have to take an additional summer-school course or switch to another language. The only problem with switching was that we were required to take two years of a language and

I wasn't too thrilled about starting over with a new language.

At Ballet Theatre School we had another nondancing course. It was a class in dance notation, a kind of shorthand writing used to show the steps in a ballet. It is very useful for learning the steps in a new ballet, like taking notes in class at school to study at home. Our teacher was one of the choreologists from the company. A choreologist is someone who records the company ballets as they are being taught, so the dancers have a permanent record of their work. When they forget steps, they come to her and she helps them.

Dance notation was interesting at first. It uses a lot of little squiggily lines that represent things like raising a foot or an arm or turning a hand. Then we had to try and put it all together very quickly. Somehow we managed to learn part of a ballet called *Con-*

At Professional Children's School, we had frequent conferences.

certo. We realized it would take years of study to be good enough at notation to use it for ourselves, but the school wanted us to at least have a familiarity with it.

I felt really lucky with all the opportunities I was given to study and perform. Everyone I knew said I had it made, but I wasn't so sure. It's a very tricky thing. Even if you get into the corps of the first company, it can be bad for you. You have to be certain that you are ready technically. And unless you go into the corps as practically soloist material, you can get stuck there for the rest of your dancing life. Also, once chosen for the corps, a dancer only gets one ballet class a day. There is no chance to go elsewhere for classes because that person is involved as an understudy in most of the day's rehearsals and sometimes into the evening.

I know this may sound crazy, but I was beginning to feel like life was passing me by and I would soon be considered old. Many of the best dancers are in a company by the time they are fifteen or sixteen. I was already fourteen and knew I had a long way to go before I could even be considered corps material. My technique had improved, and I owed a lot of that to Mr. Prinz and Miss Wilde. Mr. Prinz would not let me get away with being weak, and when I was completely down on myself Miss Widle would encourage me.

One of the main reasons I felt old was that Miss Wilde was auditioning all over the country for the new ABT school summer program, and the students being considered were almost all around thirteen and fourteen. I had been the youngest in the class and was given a lot of extra attention. But suddenly I knew I was not going to be the baby anymore, and that quite

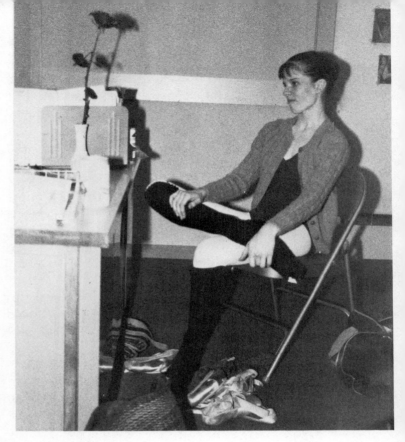

Everyone I knew said I had it made, but I wasn't so sure.

possibly I could be pushed out completely by this new
talent. The administrator had a whole file of pictures,
and the girls really looked good.

After these girls had auditioned, they had taken
company classes, and some of them were real favorites. It was true that I had been a favorite also, but
these were fresh new faces and they had legs as long
as mine and just as much training behind them. I was
scared about the summer. Not only was I worried

about the new students but I was also afraid the school was going to fold.

Even though everyone in administration went on as if the school would continue in the fall, no one was certain. We kept asking what would become of us. I knew I had to have at least one more year of training. If I couldn't get it at Ballet Theatre, I would have to think about other choices.

Since I already had my New York apartment, I wouldn't have to move back to New Jersey. If my ABT program folded, I would probably try to get back into School of American Ballet. But I wondered whether they would take me back. I had to have a full scholarship because my parents couldn't afford both an apartment and ballet tuition. But no one had said anything yet about the school definitely closing, so I tried to pretend it wasn't a problem and continue as if I would go there for another year.

I don't think I could have left New York City even if I had to. The city was now as much a part of me as dance. Now that I was going to Lincoln Center almost every night, New York was a way of life for me. In the middle of the season, American Ballet Theatre had a gala performance and afterward there was a big party at the Red Parrot, which is one of the biggest discos in the city. It was absolutely wild, with crowds of people, two bands, and huge cages with live exotic birds. Everyone who was connected with the ballet world was there and I felt like a celebrity.

Ellie and I took a taxi home when it was over. We always took a cab when it was late. The later it gets, the more unsafe the city is. I've been lucky never to have had anything bad happen to me, but that is also probably because I am very careful. I make a point always to be with several people and never go into a dangerous part of town. You really have to keep up your guard in New York City. People seem to know when you don't, and that's when trouble can happen.

It's also important to watch what you wear. I love miniskirts, but I won't wear them in the street. There are too many creepy men around and they won't leave you alone if you are dressed too attractively or suggestively. Even when the weather is hot and muggy, I try to stay covered up as much as possible. It's better to be a little bit too warm than to be followed and annoyed by some weirdo. It's not only scary to have that happen, it's also embarrassing.

Ellie seemed to be getting the feeling that she would not be part of the new school program even if there was one. She had injured her heel and was unable to dance for two months. When she came back to classes, it was very difficult for her. I hoped she would stay because I didn't want to lose her as a roommate. She and I got along beautifully.

Ellie and I had fun trying to cook. I say "trying" to cook because neither one of us was very good at fixing anything. Our biggest success was usually a frozen dinner cooked in the microwave oven, and we even messed those up sometimes.

When spring was in full bloom, we had one more outing to the Cloisters. After this tour we had to go back to the studio for an afternoon class. All morning we whined about having to go back, but by the time we finished the tour we wanted a class and would have been disappointed if it had been canceled. Our attitude had really changed. All the extra classes we took gave us more energy and made us want to dance all the more. I had been lucky not to get injured much. Except for the knee injury in modern class and the back injury when we rehearsed *Valse Fantasy*, I

I had my own room where I could just be alone with my thoughts.

had one other injury that was memorable not because it was bad but because of what happened.

During one class, my knee began to hurt and felt like it was going to slip out of the socket. I got scared and limped into the hallway. As usual, I thought I had ruined myself for life, and I sat on the hall bench crying and holding my knee. Suddenly someone sat beside me and asked what was wrong. I looked up and saw Misha! Trying desperately to pull myself together, I told him I had hurt my knee. I still couldn't stop crying. He gave me a really sympathetic look and told me to come upstairs with him. We were outside his office and he sent someone to get a chemical ice pack for me. Evidently he had been on his way to a rehearsal and was in a hurry, because when he got the pack he tried to break the inner bag and when it wouldn't break, he got impatient with it and pounded it on the floor. By this time I had stopped crying because I couldn't believe that he would take time to help me like that.

When he finally got the pack to break so the chemicals would make it cold, he handed it to me and told his secretary to let me lie down on the sofa of his office until my knee felt better. Then he ran off to rehearsal. I don't think I even felt my knee after that, especially when I was lying there in his office looking at all the pictures. I still don't believe it all ever happened.

After the company finished its New York season, a large group went to Europe. The studios became very quiet. Our own summer program was supposed to begin the day after the Fourth of July. We all wanted to celebrate the end of our year but we weren't sure whether it or not to celebrate. Rumors were thick that the school would fold at the end of the summer. We felt guilty because we thought if the school did close, maybe it was our fault for not being good enough.

But we *were* good, considering what we had looked like at the beginning of the year, a ragged bunch of undisciplined students in sweatsuits. We had not only learned the lecture demonstration pieces like *Corsair* and *Don Quixote*, but we also learned many other difficult pas de deux pieces. In our variations classes we had learned a lot more dances, not to mention dance notation, some art history, and a beginning knowledge of modern dance. We had performed all over the city and were still in demand for future performances. The American Ballet Theatre School had become something like a third company to Ballet Theatre, and just as it had begun to come alive, it looked like it was going to be stopped.

We had all improved considerably and looked better than we had at the beginning of the year.

On July 2nd, I did something really dumb. It was common for all of us to take extra classes around the city, especially when we had a holiday. None of us liked to miss a day of class because the next day we would have sore muscles. I wanted to look especially good for the following Monday, because the school was going to videotape our class and I wanted to stand out. So I took a very difficult class at another studio that Friday and got carried away. During the center floor combinations, I slipped and sprained my ankle. I ended up celebrating the Fourth of July on crutches and was scared to death I would get in a lot of trouble when I went back to the studio.

Ellie and I did have fun on the Fourth. We went to the top of the Empire State Building to watch the fireworks. Since I was on crutches, the people let me go up front to the railing so I could see better. The fireworks were over the Hudson River and they lasted about a half-hour. The Empire State Building was all lit up with red, white, and blue lights. It was times like these that I especially loved New York City, times when you could share a holiday with thousands of strangers and feel at home with them.

I went to the studio Monday morning with an elastic bandage on my foot. The injury was not serious, but it had to be babied for a few days. I was frantic because I knew Miss Wilde was angry because I took an outside class and hurt myself and couldn't participate in the videotape.

I sat during the class and watched the new students. It was really interesting, because I could compare the old scholarship students to the new ones. The new ones didn't seem so threatening anymore. Some of them were very good and some of them had incredible bodies, but most of them had lots of the bad habits we had spent all year trying to get rid of.

There was this one girl who was a beautiful dancer but she had a slight swayback. Since that throws off the hips, I don't know how she managed to do anything at all. I saw lots of my own bad habits in others and realized why Mr. Prinz used to get so angry with me.

I realized something else by watching. We had all been lucky to have had such a small class all year. Now there were forty students in each class. It was kind of a nightmare, especially before class when the new ones would run in and grab all the good barre spaces. Some of them even tied leg warmers around the barres to save their places. Center floor was a mess because it was too crowded to dance full out. Ballet Theatre summer class was not so different from anywhere else in New York now—crowded and competitive. The competition woke up most of the full-year students and that was good for us, but we sure hated crowds. We were spoiled from having only twelve in a class.

The rumor that the school was closing was no longer a rumor. It was true. It was definitely going to close at the end of the summer, and everyone was crazy over it, even the new students, because some of them had given up valuable scholarships to come to Ballet Theatre School. My situation was not as serious as that of the older students who still needed additional training, especially the boys. Ballet schools were beginning to be flooded with talented boys. Boys did not have as much of an advantage as they had several years before, when they could name their school. Younger boys were getting the scholarships now, some of them as young as eleven.

Smaller regional companies wanted all of us, but we did not want second best. All of us wanted to be in American Ballet Theatre, New York City Ballet, or Joffrey, and we knew we needed more training. What we really wanted was for ABT school not to fold. If we had to leave ABT, we wouldn't be able to work with their superstars anymore. I had been one of the lucky students chosen by Johan Renvall to work with him in a new dance he was choreographing. He worked with us after hours in one of the empty studios and he even taught us a Russian pas de deux that had never been performed in the United States. It was extremely complicated and had a fast girl's variation. He demonstrated it for us and asked if anyone wanted to try it.

I don't think Johan liked me at the beginning of the year. He seemed to think I was not interesting and couldn't do anything. So the day Johan wanted one of us to try the variation, I volunteered. Then he said we were going to run through the whole thing! I was scared, but somehow I got through it and finished with fourteen fouetté turns. These are a series of turns you do while rising up and down on the toe of the other foot. I think he was impressed, and I was very pleased with myself and a little surprised too. I wondered if Johan would ever dance with me as a real pas de deux partner.

We used to wonder about partners a lot. On our breaks we would go watch company rehearsals and try to decide whom we'd like as a partner. Sometimes company members would come in and watch our

classes, and I wondered if they were thinking the same thing.

During the third week of the summer program, a group of us went over to School of American Ballet for a special audition. I was worried they wouldn't take me because I had turned them down. A lot of the others worried about this too. I was very worried for Ellie because if they didn't accept her she would have to go back to California and I wouldn't have her for a roommate anymore.

The audition was not very long. They made us do a few things, and most of us didn't warm up very well. Personally, I had not been so frightened of an audition since the time I went to SAB with a warning from Mom that if I didn't make it I would have to quit dance. I knew that wouldn't happen, but I really wanted to go to SAB this time.

After we did pirouettes, we were told thank you and asked to come into the office one at a time. The first few who went in came out in tears. One of them was Ellie. She didn't make it, and I couldn't have felt worse if it had been me.

I got in, but didn't know whether or not I would have a scholarship. One of the boys who got in kept bragging and wouldn't shut up. He didn't seem to notice that the ones who weren't chosen didn't want to hear how wonderful he thought he was. I didn't know what to say to Ellie to make her feel better. Even though I was relieved at being accepted, I couldn't be very excited about it and hoped Ellie would find a way to stay anyway. We cried a lot that night.

The only good thing at the time was that at least I knew where I would be the following year. I wouldn't

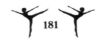

get as many classes per day, but the training would be excellent and I would still be seen by the important people at American Ballet Theatre because School of American Ballet is where a lot of their dancers came from.

I was sad to be leaving all my friends from the year's scholarship class. Only one of the boys was going to SAB. Everyone else was going elsewhere. A few of them got contracts to the second company, but no one felt the same about anything anymore.

Ellie was definitely going back to California and I made arrangements for a new roommate. I didn't know this new girl very well and was not sure how things would work out. My worst fear was living in a situation like the one I had been in during the summer I first came to American Ballet Theatre. But I guess life goes on, and the most important thing to me was staying in New York and studying at School of American Ballet.

As the summer course drew to an end, we prepared to do a two-week workshop with the second company. American Ballet Theatre School—after being in existence for over thirty years—was gone. Patricia Wilde, the director, had a new job as the artistic director for the Pittsburgh Ballet Theatre, and John Prinz was talking about opening his own school.

We were given a giant catered party on the last official day of school. All day long, cases of champagne and exotic food arrived. Most of us tried not to think about what it all meant, that we would never be together like this as a family again. It was more emotional than a graduation because there were so few of us.

But we had a wonderful party with lots of hugs and promises to get together. Misha even sat down with

Miss Wilde and I posed for a picture at the party on the last day of classes at American Ballet Theatre.

When I talked to Misha, I laughed mostly from nerves.

me before the celebration and asked about my future
plans. I mostly just laughed from nerves.

My future? I don't know what it will bring, and I
don't care as long as it includes dance. I want to be a
ballerina and I *will* be if it is the only thing I ever do. I
have at least two more years of training ahead of me
until the critical moment. That moment will mean
either I will be accepted as a promising ballerina or I
will be told to find something else to do with my life.
But I have to succeed and I *will* succeed, because I am
a survivor.

Epilogue

Shane and Melissa are both realists. They are no longer children who believe ballet is a few classes, a starring role in the *Nutcracker,* or meeting a superstar.

They have seen ballet at its best at a much younger age than most students. Both of them know what it is like to be onstage at the Metropolitan Opera House and to take classes with the best dancers in the world.

Shane and Melissa have also experienced New York City life in different ways. Most students don't have as many problems as Shane, but not too many of them have it as easy as Melissa.

As far as the careers of these teenagers, they both have a great deal in their favor. Opportunities have fallen into both their lives that some students would give anything to have.

One thing has to be remembered. There are thousands of other students who have tried to come to New York and be a success, and they got nowhere. Even the students who have been more successful than Shane and Melissa do not always make it to the top.

So far, Shane and Melissa have the right bodies and a lot of excellent training. Even with all this they still have to push their way ahead of the children of those who know important and influential people. If Shane and Melissa succeed, they still have to be careful they don't get an injury that will force them to stop dancing. A twenty-year-old ballerina usually has the feet

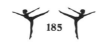

of a fifty-year-old who has never danced. Men dancers in their twenties often have weakened backs and knees.

Melissa doesn't just want to dance. She has only one goal—to be a classical ballerina and be accepted by one of the big companies. She might consider going to Europe to dance if an American company won't take her. Melissa says her attitude will help her succeed. She wants to be a principal dancer and she will accept nothing less. To accomplish this, she needs to develop a special quality that comes with maturity. It is the difference between just doing ballet steps and feeling the ballet inside. That feeling is translated to the audience. Without a soul and personality that shines through, a dancer can expect to always remain in the corps.

Melissa went on to the School of American Ballet and continued her classes. She still misses American Ballet Theatre, but is beginning to love her new life. Now she watches the superstars at New York City Ballet while they rehearse in other rooms.

Melissa's life is going right according to her plans. She is well liked and continues to improve. Perhaps someday all her dreams will come true.

Shane has given himself a few more choices in life. When he first came to New York City, he felt very much the same way as Melissa—that ballet was all he would study. Ballet is and probably always will be his first love in the arts. But he has problems with his feet and he has to work twice as hard for what some boys have naturally, like nice arches and limber legs. He may also not grow tall enough for a major company.

Like Melissa, Shane will not settle for stardom in a small regional company. If he is in a ballet company, it has to be one of the best. But the difference between

Hopefully someday Melissa and Shane will see their dreams come true.

187

the two is that Shane is willing to look beyond ballet. He is even looking beyond the arts if he has to. He has already sold his Atari and bought a computer. He is also thinking about college. He knows the artistic life of a dancer does not last much beyond thirty. At that age he would have to quit dance and do something else. With no schooling, the only thing he could do would be to teach or choreograph. He can't see himself as a teacher and does not think he would have the talent for choreography.

Shane went on to Salt Lake City and is taking classes with the school for Ballet West. At first, he was not sure he liked his new classes, but now he feels he is getting a great deal of technical help from his teachers. He still has every intention of returning to New York City, but he may first take a summer course in Texas from Mr. Joffrey himself.

Shane was worried about going back into public school and having to deal with all the old problems of classmates teasing him, but so far even that is not so bad. His schedule is arranged so he can leave early for his dance classes.

Dance is not Shane's only subject now. He is talking about learning to drive and what kind of a car he wants when he is old enough to have one. He is also anxiously awaiting the ski season at Park City, which is only an hour from where he lives.

Shane still wants to accomplish something big, but he is not as frantic about it anymore. As far as he is concerned, if things work out for him in dance, that is terrific. If they don't, there are always other things in life. But no matter what, Shane will never forget Lincoln Center and he will always be more than a little in love with the big stage.

INDEX

ABOUT THE AUTHOR

Alexandra Collard has danced most of her life—modern, tap, and classical ballet. She also has been an actress, folk singer, and race car driver, and has an MA degree in Clinical Psychology.

In addition, Ms. Collard has worked as an administrative assistant for the School of American Ballet and Administrator of American Ballet Theatre School, both in New York City. She currently lives in San Diego with her husband, Tom Hohing, and daughter, Stephanie. Ms. Collard is Shane Gregory's mother.